The Zen of the Labyrinth

The Zen of the Labyrinth

MAZES FOR THE CONNOISSEUR

■ ■ ■

Dave Phillips

PUZZLE WRIGHT PRESS

An imprint of Sterling
Publishing Co., Inc.

www.puzzlewright.com

Puzzlewright Press and the distinctive Puzzlewright Press logo are trademarks of
Sterling Publishing Co., Inc.

10 9 8 7 6 5 4 3 2 1

Published by Sterling Publishing Co., Inc.
387 Park Avenue South, New York, NY 10016
© 2009 by Dave Phillips
Distributed in Canada by Sterling Publishing
c/o Canadian Manda Group, 165 Dufferin Street
Toronto, Ontario, Canada M6K 3H6
Distributed in the United Kingdom by GMC Distribution Services
Castle Place, 166 High Street, Lewes, East Sussex, England BN7 1XU
Distributed in Australia by Capricorn Link (Australia) Pty. Ltd.
P.O. Box 704, Windsor, NSW 2756, Australia

Designed by Celia Fuller

Sterling ISBN 978-1-4027-5987-1

For information about custom editions, special sales, premium and
corporate purchases, please contact Sterling Special Sales
Department at 800-805-5489 or specialsales@sterlingpublishing.com.

CONTENTS

INTRODUCTION

A maze is a confusing jumble of branching, twisting paths defined by walls. Whether the walls are real, made of stone or hedge, or are simply black lines printed on a flat page, they are forbidden territory. We accept from childhood the rule of drawing a pencil line within a maze without crossing a black-line wall. For a printed maze to continue to challenge a maturing intellect, however, more and more paths are required, defined by more and more walls.

Starting at the exit of a maze and going backwards to the entrance is a popular trick for solving a maze more easily. Working this way defeats many deceptions designed by the maze-maker. A clever designer may counter this cheat, however, by crafting the maze to be equally challenging from both directions. This design ploy requires more paths (approaching twice as many), in order to maintain the difficulty level experienced by the solver who dutifully starts from the start and ends at the end.

A maze explorer wanders down a dead-end path only to the point of realizing the futility of continuing further. The greater the ability of the solver to see ahead, the longer and more convoluted a dead end must be to fool the eye, requiring yet more paths and walls. A well-designed maze of looped paths (containing no dead ends), however, may lead the solver unknowingly back to the start. At some point, though, even a well-designed printed maze becomes either too tedious or too easy to entice the interest of people beyond childhood. It has either too many paths or too few. That is only true, however, if we adhere solely to that first rule of staying within the lines.

This collection of puzzle mazes adds a few more rules of movement to the basic concept of the maze. By so doing, the number of paths and walls are kept to an almost absurd minimum. The puzzles are designed to draw you in with simple, bold graphics, fooling you into thinking they are not so tough; they are, however, meant to entertain and challenge adult puzzle enthusiasts. No one will find them trivial.

Your goal is to discover the solution path for each maze by using logic and deduction. Feel free to work the maze forward, backward, or from any point at all.

There are eight sections in the book. Each section contains a unique set of rules and twenty puzzles, organized more or less in ascending order of difficulty. Retracing paths is allowed in the first four sections, but is prohibited in the last four sections. Overall rules are given here in the introduction (at right). Individual section goals and rules are located at the beginning of each section, along with solving tips. Shortened versions of the goal and rules for each section are included below each maze, as a reminder.

Solutions are provided at the back of the book so that you can check them if you become convinced that a puzzle is impossible. Have fun!

OVERALL RULES

All puzzle mazes in this collection share the following rule: Black areas are forbidden.

Sections 1 through 4 (Color Path, Straight, Flow, and Turns): Retracing your path is allowed (and often required). The solutions in the back of the book omit useless loops.

Sections 5 through 8 (Sequence A, Sequence B, Two in a Row, and Looped): Paths may be used only once. In this way, you will make your own dead ends when passing through an intersection.

Color Path

GOAL: If the maze has a center gray square, enter by the bottom red path and end on the center gray square. If the maze has an exit along the top, enter by the bottom red path and exit from the top of the maze.

RULES: You may retrace your path but you may not make a U-turn on a pathway. You must follow the paths in the order red, blue, yellow and then red, blue, yellow again, as needed, changing color on the white squares.

HINTS: There are no traps. Some solutions require revisiting some paths twice and revisiting some squares as many as three times.

Color Path 1

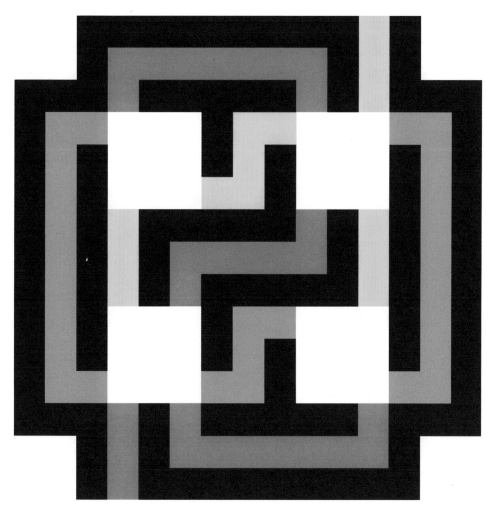

GOAL: Enter from the bottom; exit by the top.

RULES: You may retrace your path. Follow paths in the order red, blue, yellow.

Color Path 2

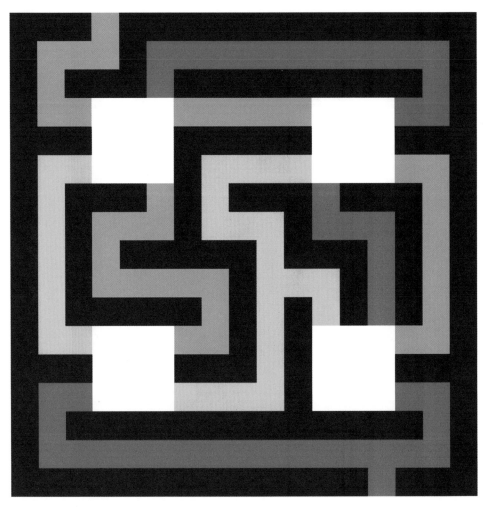

GOAL: Enter from the bottom; exit by the top.

RULES: You may retrace your path. Follow paths in the order red, blue, yellow.

Color Path 3

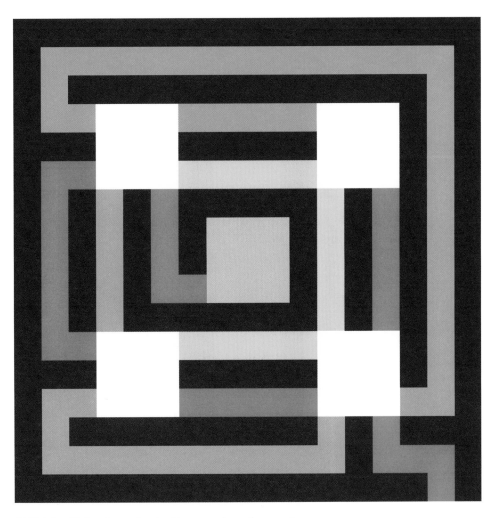

GOAL: Enter from the bottom; end on the center gray square.

RULES: You may retrace your path. Follow paths in the order red, blue, yellow.

Color Path 4

GOAL: Enter from the bottom; exit by the top.

RULES: You may retrace your path. Follow paths in the order red, blue, yellow.

Color Path 5

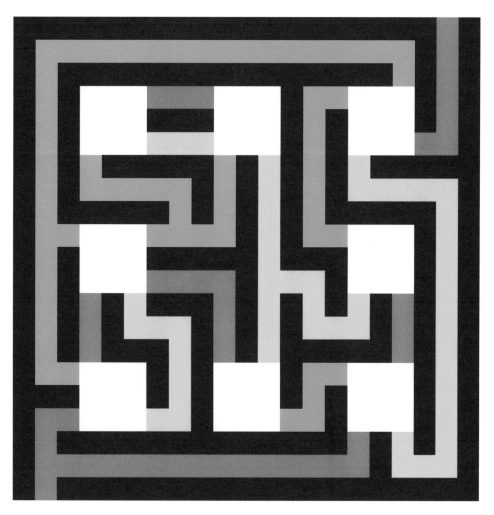

GOAL: Enter from the bottom; exit by the top.
RULES: You may retrace your path. Follow paths in the order red, blue, yellow.

Color Path 6

GOAL: Enter from the bottom; exit by the top.

RULES: You may retrace your path. Follow paths in the order red, blue, yellow.

Color Path 7

GOAL: Enter from the bottom; end on the center gray square.
RULES: You may retrace your path. Follow paths in the order red, blue, yellow.

11

Color Path 8

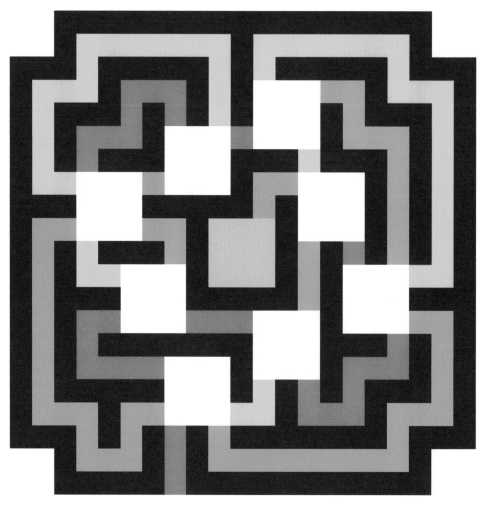

GOAL: Enter from the bottom; end on the center gray square.

RULES: You may retrace your path. Follow paths in the order red, blue, yellow.

Color Path 9

GOAL: Enter from the bottom; exit by the top.

RULES: You may retrace your path. Follow paths in the order red, blue, yellow.

Color Path 10

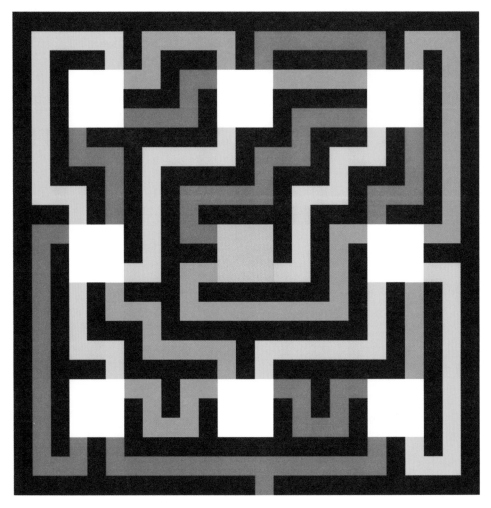

GOAL: Enter from the bottom; end on the center gray square.

RULES: You may retrace your path. Follow paths in the order red, blue, yellow.

Color Path 11

GOAL: Enter from the bottom; end on the center gray square.

RULES: You may retrace your path. Follow paths in the order red, blue, yellow.

Color Path 12

GOAL: Enter from the bottom; exit by the top.

RULES: You may retrace your path. Follow paths in the order red, blue, yellow.

Color Path 13

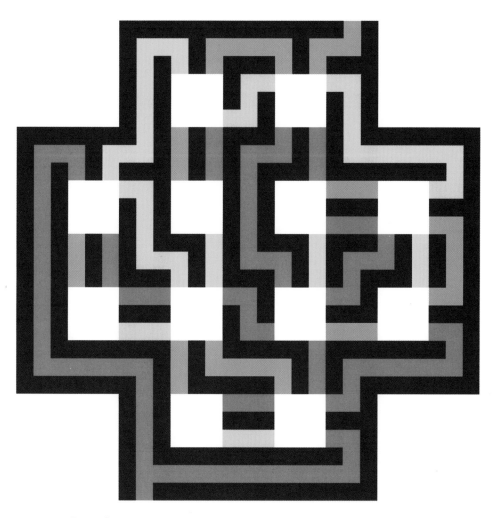

GOAL: Enter from the bottom; exit by the top.

RULES: You may retrace your path. Follow paths in the order red, blue, yellow.

Color Path 14

GOAL: Enter from the bottom; exit by the top.
RULES: You may retrace your path. Follow paths in the order red, blue, yellow.

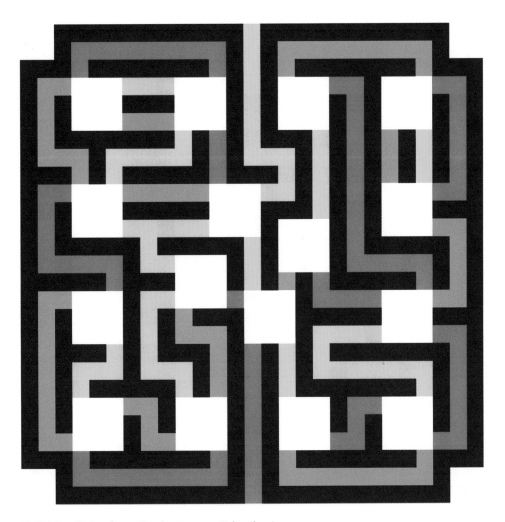

GOAL: Enter from the bottom; exit by the top.

RULES: You may retrace your path. Follow paths in the order red, blue, yellow.

Color Path 16

GOAL: Enter from the bottom; exit by the top.
RULES: You may retrace your path. Follow paths in the order red, blue, yellow.

Color Path 17

GOAL: Enter from the bottom; exit by the top.

RULES: You may retrace your path. Follow paths in the order red, blue, yellow.

Color Path 18

GOAL: Enter from the bottom; exit by the top.
RULES: You may retrace your path. Follow paths in the order red, blue, yellow.

GOAL: Enter from the bottom; end on the center gray square.
RULES: You may retrace your path. Follow paths in the order red, blue, yellow.

Color Path 20

GOAL: Enter from the bottom; end on the center gray square.
RULES: You may retrace your path. Follow paths in the order red, blue, yellow.

Straight

GOAL: Draw a single path that enters at the perimeter of the maze, passes through all blue squares, and then leaves the maze.

RULES: You may retrace your paths. Follow along the nonblack tiles horizontally or vertically in a straight line until a black wall forces a turn. When forced to turn, you may choose either direction. (You may also return back in the direction you came, though of course, as usual, you may not stop until you reach a wall.) If you do not encounter a black wall, you must continue out of the maze. A maze is solved only when all blue squares have been visited at least once before leaving the maze.

HINTS: Many tiles require two visits, some even require three. Try to deduce the location of the entrance and exit. Sometimes a blue square can only be visited by way of the first or last move.

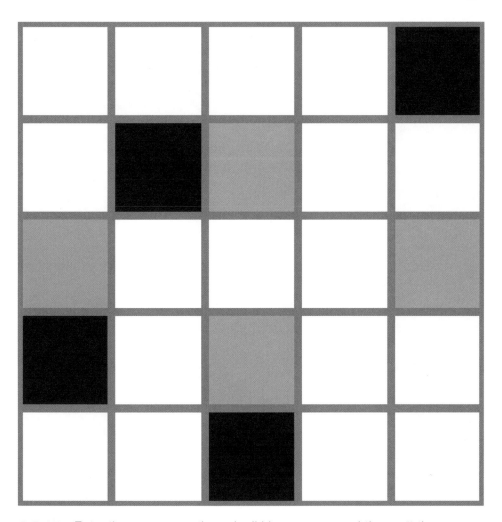

GOAL: Enter the maze, pass through all blue squares, and then exit the maze.

RULES: You may retrace your path. Go straight unless forced to turn.

Straight 2

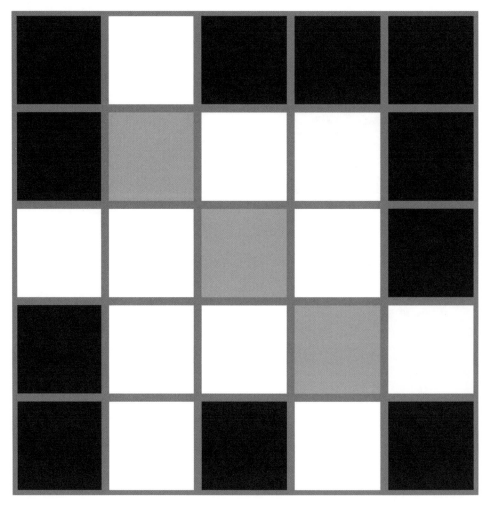

GOAL: Enter the maze, pass through all blue squares, and then exit the maze.

RULES: You may retrace your path. Go straight unless forced to turn.

Straight 3

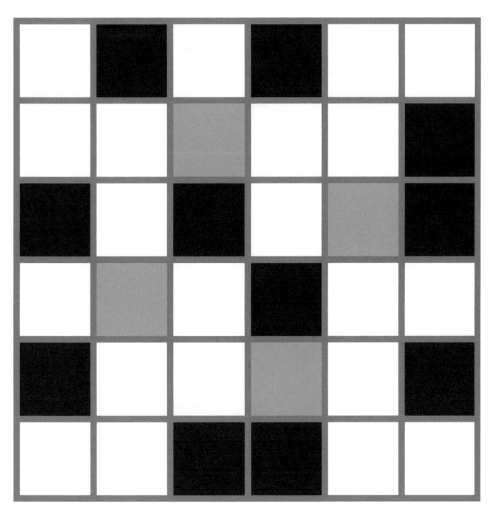

GOAL: Enter the maze, pass through all blue squares, and then exit the maze.

RULES: You may retrace your path. Go straight unless forced to turn.

Straight 4

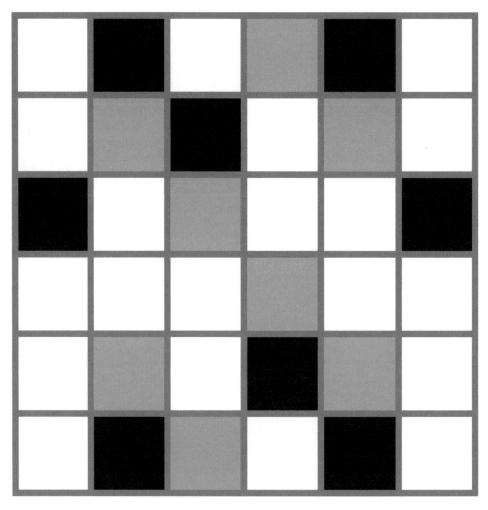

GOAL: Enter the maze, pass through all blue squares, and then exit the maze.

RULES: You may retrace your path. Go straight unless forced to turn.

Straight 5

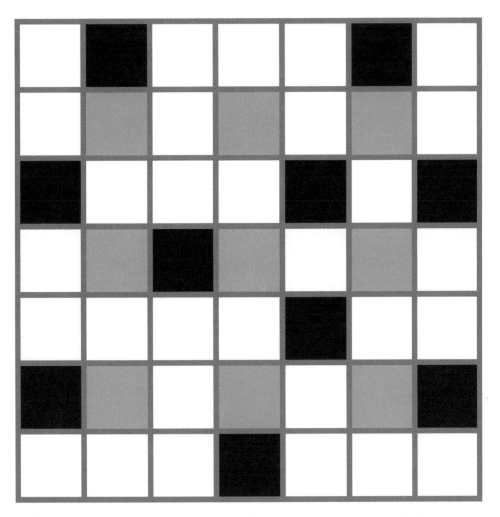

GOAL: Enter the maze, pass through all blue squares, and then exit the maze.

RULES: You may retrace your path. Go straight unless forced to turn.

Straight 6

GOAL: Enter the maze, pass through all blue squares, and then exit the maze.

RULES: You may retrace your path. Go straight unless forced to turn.

Straight 7

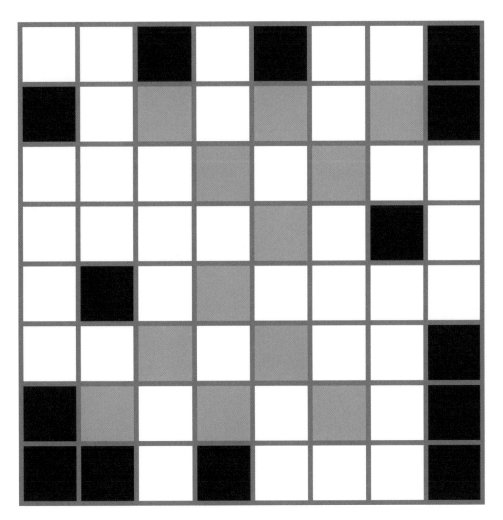

GOAL: Enter the maze, pass through all blue squares, and then exit the maze.

RULES: You may retrace your path. Go straight unless forced to turn.

Straight 8

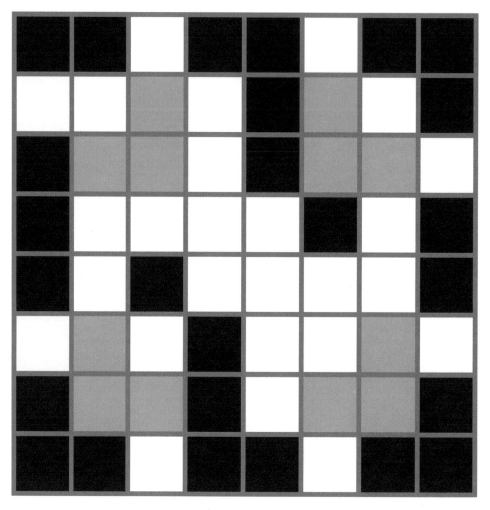

GOAL: Enter the maze, pass through all blue squares, and then exit the maze.

RULES: You may retrace your path. Go straight unless forced to turn.

34

Straight 9

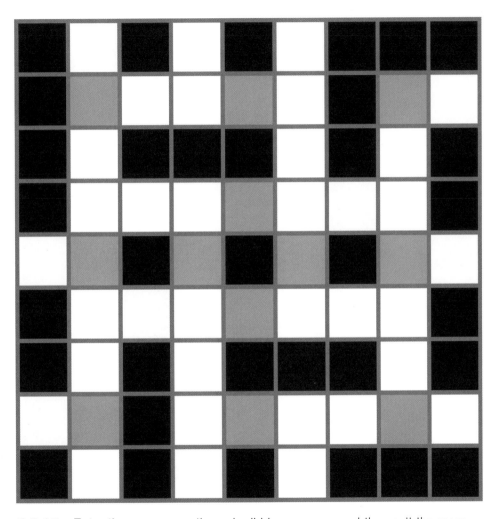

GOAL: Enter the maze, pass through all blue squares, and then exit the maze.

RULES: You may retrace your path. Go straight unless forced to turn.

Straight 10

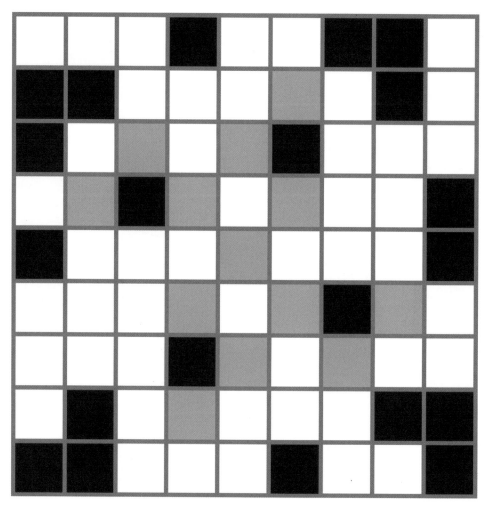

GOAL: Enter the maze, pass through all blue squares, and then exit the maze.

RULES: You may retrace your path. Go straight unless forced to turn.

Straight 11

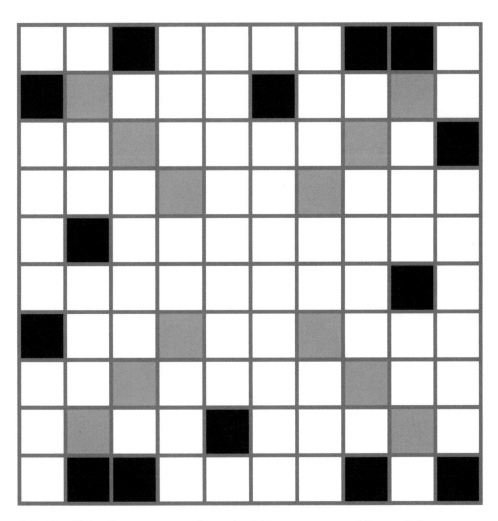

GOAL: Enter the maze, pass through all blue squares, and then exit the maze.

RULES: You may retrace your path. Go straight unless forced to turn.

Straight 12

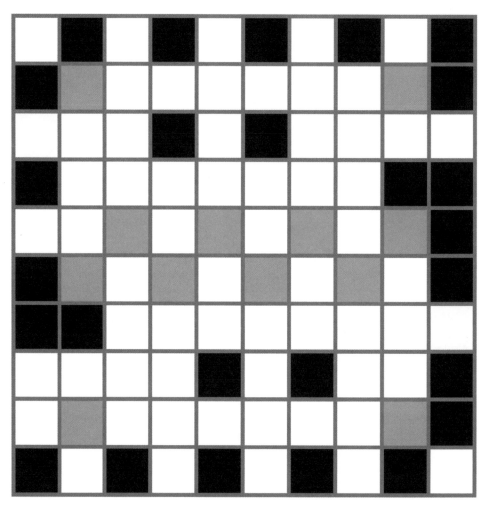

GOAL: Enter the maze, pass through all blue squares, and then exit the maze.

RULES: You may retrace your path. Go straight unless forced to turn.

Straight 13

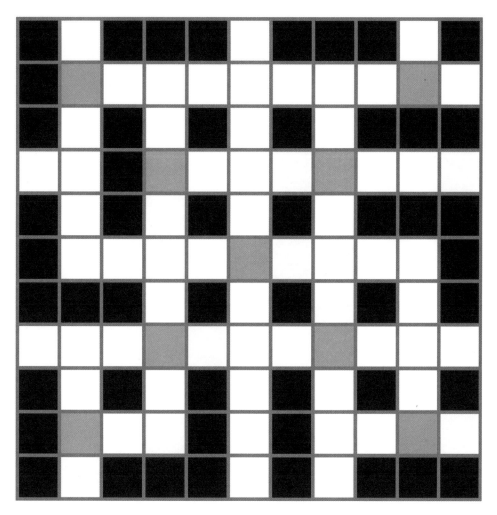

GOAL: Enter the maze, pass through all blue squares, and then exit the maze.

RULES: You may retrace your path. Go straight unless forced to turn.

Straight 14

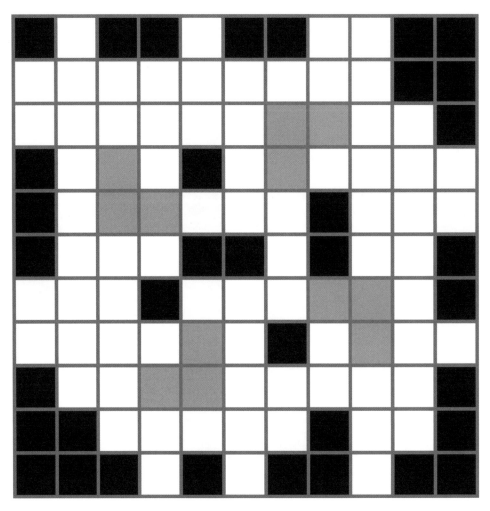

GOAL: Enter the maze, pass through all blue squares, and then exit the maze.

RULES: You may retrace your path. Go straight unless forced to turn.

Straight 15

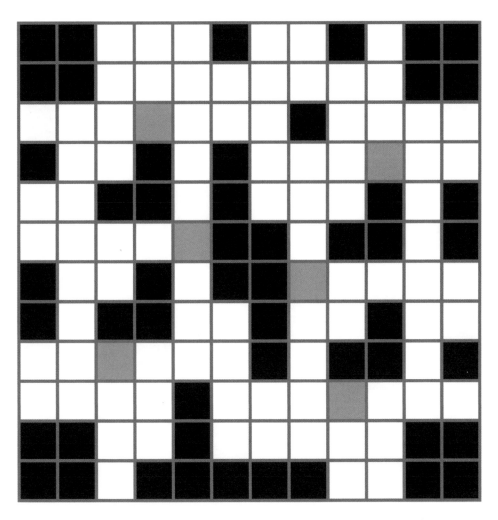

GOAL: Enter the maze, pass through all blue squares, and then exit the maze.

RULES: You may retrace your path. Go straight unless forced to turn.

Straight 16

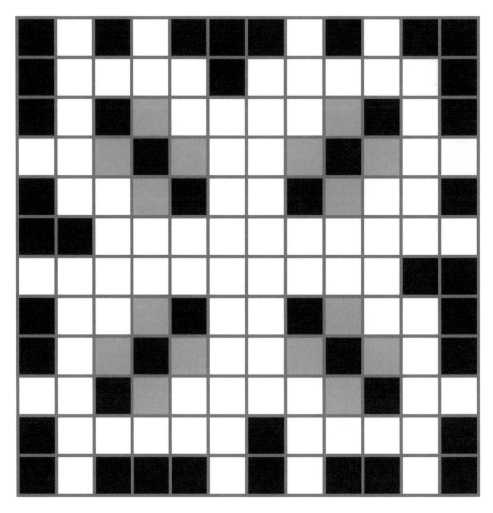

GOAL: Enter the maze, pass through all blue squares, and then exit the maze.

RULES: You may retrace your path. Go straight unless forced to turn.

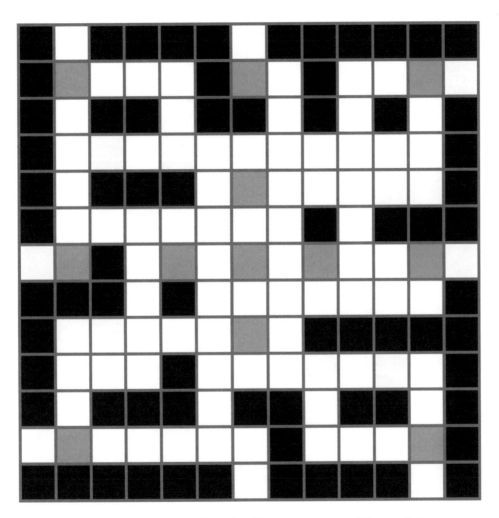

GOAL: Enter the maze, pass through all blue squares, and then exit the maze.

RULES: You may retrace your path. Go straight unless forced to turn.

Straight 18

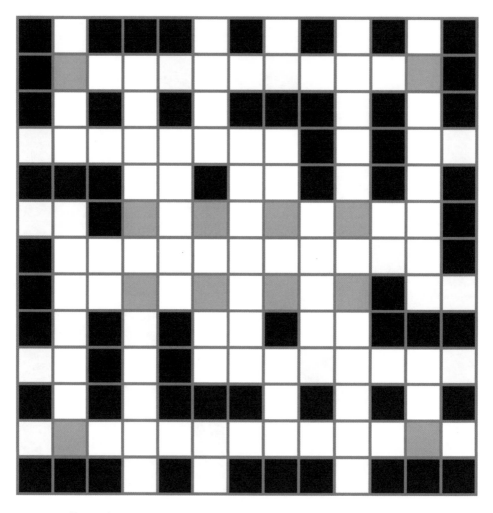

GOAL: Enter the maze, pass through all blue squares, and then exit the maze.

RULES: You may retrace your path. Go straight unless forced to turn.

Straight 19

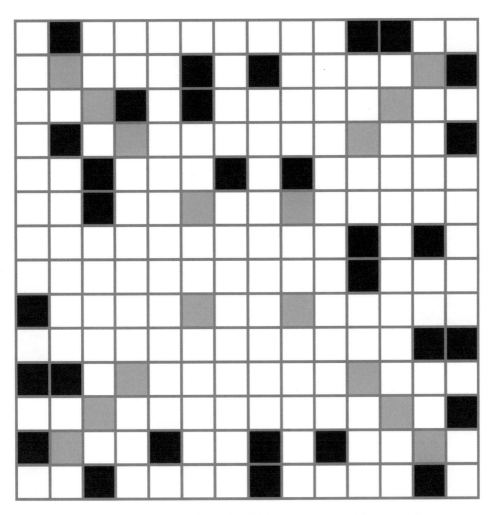

GOAL: Enter the maze, pass through all blue squares, and then exit the maze.

RULES: You may retrace your path. Go straight unless forced to turn.

Straight 20

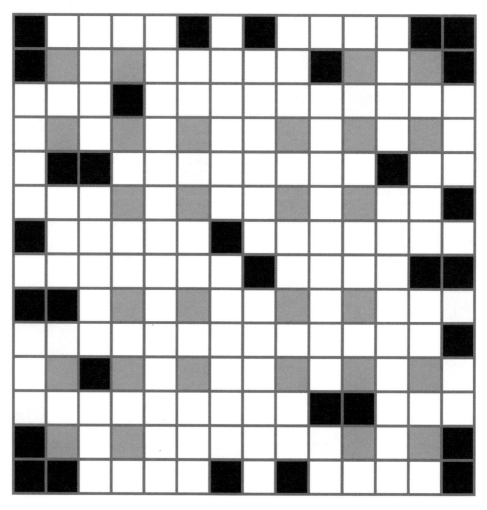

GOAL: Enter the maze, pass through all blue squares, and then exit the maze.

RULES: You may retrace your path. Go straight unless forced to turn.

Flow

GOAL: Enter the maze through any of the available entrances, pass through all yellow circles, and then exit the maze.

RULES: You may retrace your paths. Your course must follow the flow—no sharp turns (a sharp turn is anything that is 90° or more). Example: You must pass straight through an intersection of two paths that form a cross; a turn at such an intersection would be 90° and therefore illegal.

HINTS: Some solutions require revisiting paths twice. One puzzle solution requires using the same path three times. The solution path may be followed in either direction. Try to deduce the two access points of each maze. Sometimes a yellow circle can only be visited on the way in or on the way out of the maze.

GOAL: Enter the maze, pass through all yellow circles, and then exit the maze.

RULES: You may retrace your path. Go with the flow—no sharp turns.

Flow 2

GOAL: Enter the maze, pass through all yellow circles, and then exit the maze.

RULES: You may retrace your path. Go with the flow—no sharp turns.

Flow 3

GOAL: Enter the maze, pass through all yellow circles, and then exit the maze.

RULES: You may retrace your path. Go with the flow—no sharp turns.

Flow 4

GOAL: Enter the maze, pass through all yellow circles, and then exit the maze.

RULES: You may retrace your path. Go with the flow—no sharp turns.

Flow 5

GOAL: Enter the maze, pass through all yellow circles, and then exit the maze.

RULES: You may retrace your path. Go with the flow—no sharp turns.

Flow 6

GOAL: Enter the maze, pass through all yellow circles, and then exit the maze.

RULES: You may retrace your path. Go with the flow—no sharp turns.

Flow 7

GOAL: Enter the maze, pass through all yellow circles, and then exit the maze.

RULES: You may retrace your path. Go with the flow—no sharp turns.

Flow 8

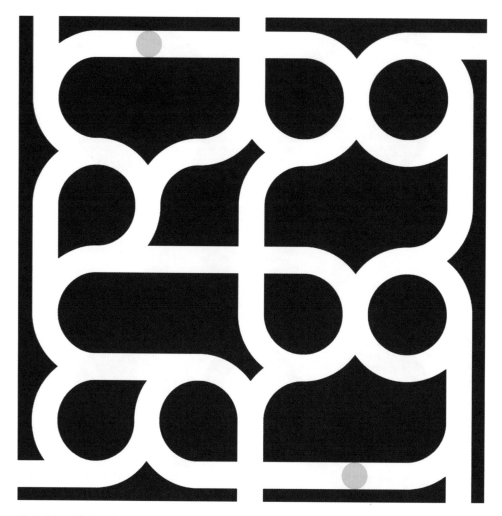

GOAL: Enter the maze, pass through all yellow circles, and then exit the maze.

RULES: You may retrace your path. Go with the flow—no sharp turns.

GOAL: Enter the maze, pass through all yellow circles, and then exit the maze.

RULES: You may retrace your path. Go with the flow—no sharp turns.

Flow 10

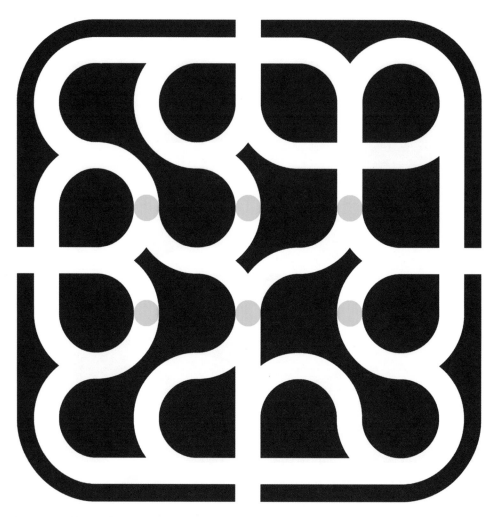

GOAL: Enter the maze, pass through all yellow circles, and then exit the maze.

RULES: You may retrace your path. Go with the flow—no sharp turns.

GOAL: Enter the maze, pass through all yellow circles, and then exit the maze.

RULES: You may retrace your path. Go with the flow—no sharp turns.

Flow 12

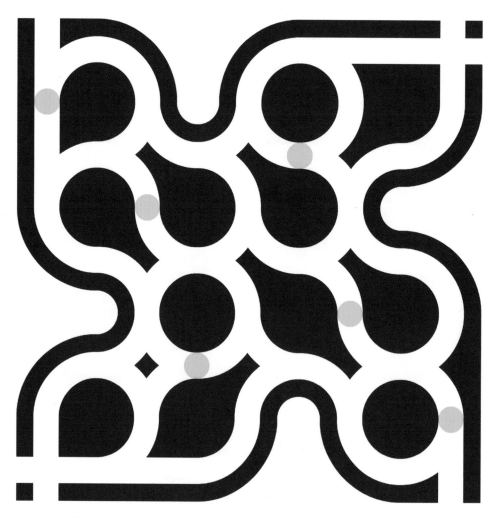

GOAL: Enter the maze, pass through all yellow circles, and then exit the maze.
RULES: You may retrace your path. Go with the flow—no sharp turns.

Flow 13

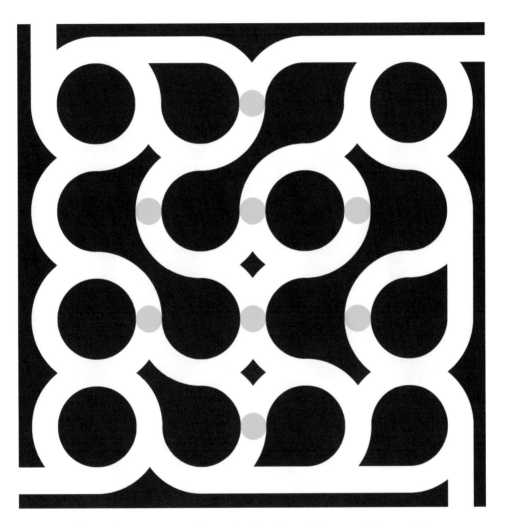

GOAL: Enter the maze, pass through all yellow circles, and then exit the maze.

RULES: You may retrace your path. Go with the flow—no sharp turns.

Flow 14

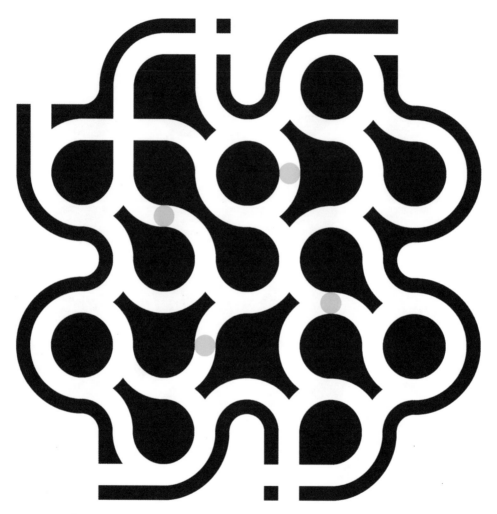

GOAL: Enter the maze, pass through all yellow circles, and then exit the maze.

RULES: You may retrace your path. Go with the flow—no sharp turns.

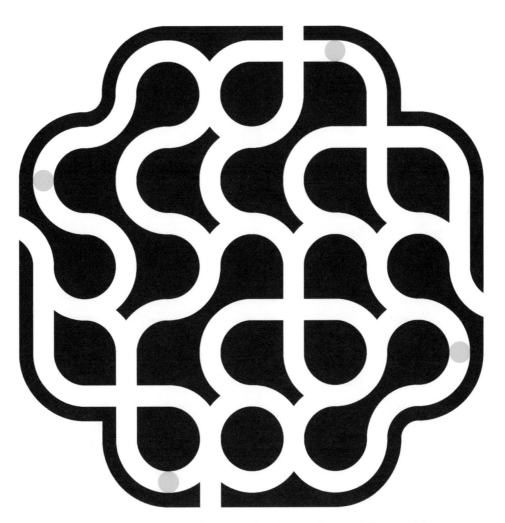

GOAL: Enter the maze, pass through all yellow circles, and then exit the maze.

RULES: You may retrace your path. Go with the flow—no sharp turns.

Flow 16

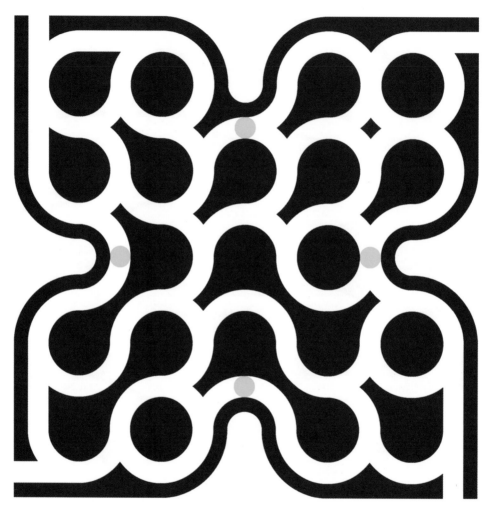

GOAL: Enter the maze, pass through all yellow circles, and then exit the maze.

RULES: You may retrace your path. Go with the flow—no sharp turns.

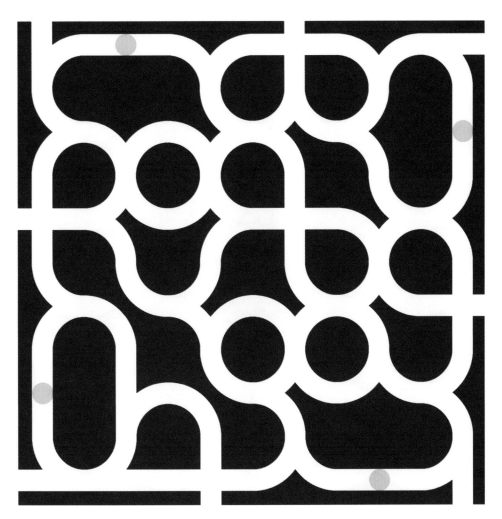

GOAL: Enter the maze, pass through all yellow circles, and then exit the maze.

RULES: You may retrace your path. Go with the flow—no sharp turns.

Flow 18

GOAL: Enter the maze, pass through all yellow circles, and then exit the maze.
RULES: You may retrace your path. Go with the flow—no sharp turns.

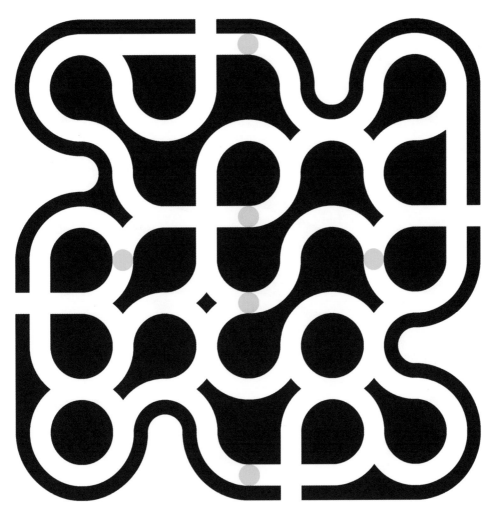

Flow 19

GOAL: Enter the maze, pass through all yellow circles, and then exit the maze.

RULES: You may retrace your path. Go with the flow—no sharp turns.

Flow 20

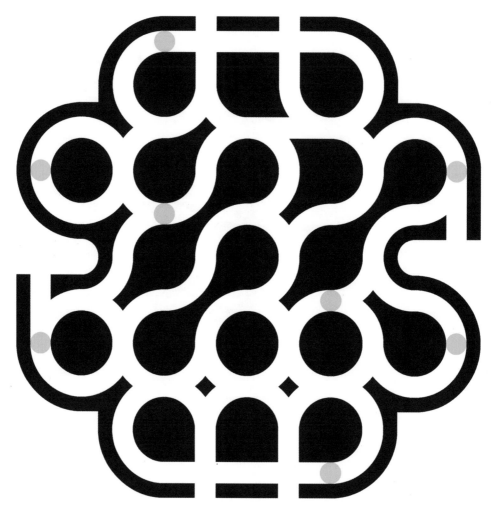

GOAL: Enter the maze, pass through all yellow circles, and then exit the maze.

RULES: You may retrace your path. Go with the flow—no sharp turns.

Turns

GOAL: Enter the maze from the bottom and exit by the top.

RULES: You may retrace your paths. When you pass over a red square, turn right immediately. When passing over a blue square, turn left immediately. When passing over a yellow square, pass straight through. You may not make a U-turn on a path. If you are forced to leave the maze by a side exit, try again. Turns refer to the point of view of the route going forward. Example: If the path is moving down the page and enters a red square from above, it should turn to the right—which means the path will then be traveling toward the left side of the page.

HINTS: Consider the maze as if you were an imaginary car following a road map, to keep from confusing the turns. You will need to visit some colored squares as many as three times and some paths twice.

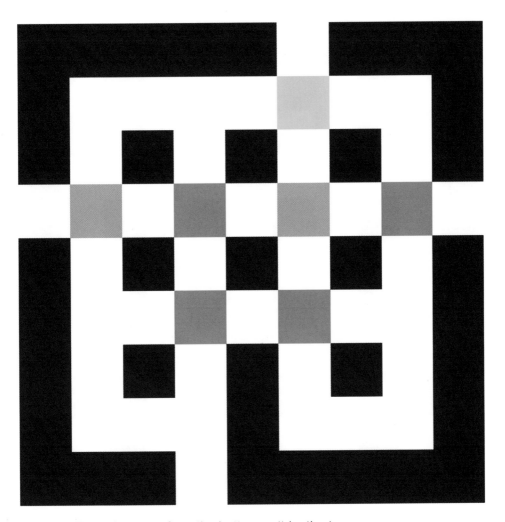

GOAL: Enter the maze from the bottom, exit by the top.
RULES: You may retrace your path. Turn right on red, turn left on blue, and go straight through yellow.

Turns 2

GOAL: Enter the maze from the bottom, exit by the top.

RULES: You may retrace your path. Turn right on red, turn left on blue, and go straight through yellow.

GOAL: Enter the maze from the bottom, exit by the top.
RULES: You may retrace your path. Turn right on red, turn left on blue, and go straight through yellow.

Turns 4

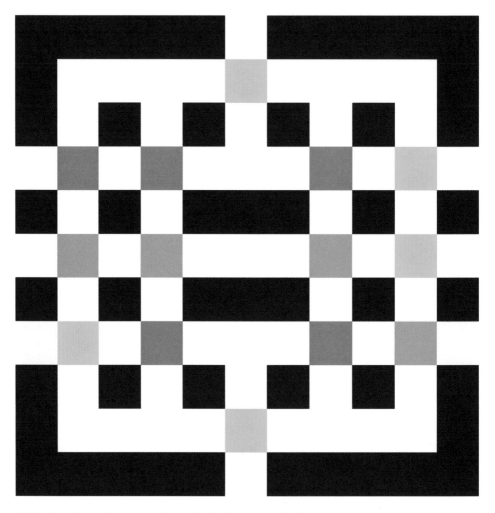

GOAL: Enter the maze from the bottom, exit by the top.
RULES: You may retrace your path. Turn right on red, turn left on blue, and go straight through yellow.

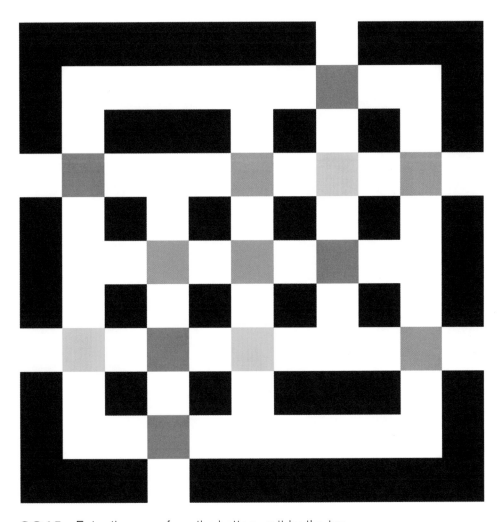

GOAL: Enter the maze from the bottom, exit by the top.
RULES: You may retrace your path. Turn right on red, turn left on blue, and go straight through yellow.

Turns 6

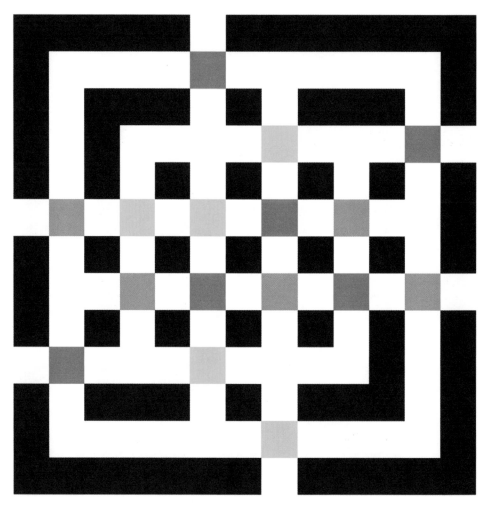

GOAL: Enter the maze from the bottom, exit by the top.
RULES: You may retrace your path. Turn right on red, turn left on blue, and go straight through yellow.

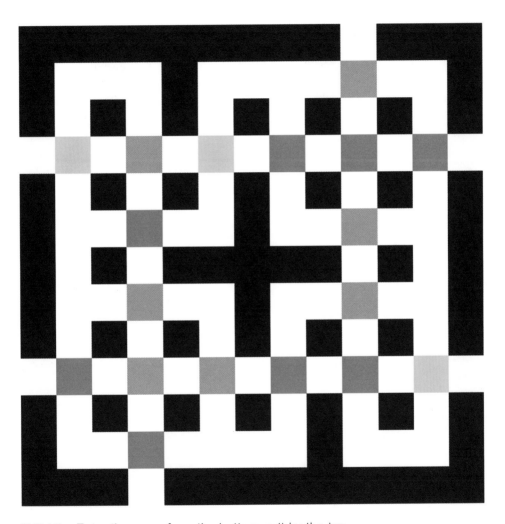

GOAL: Enter the maze from the bottom, exit by the top.
RULES: You may retrace your path. Turn right on red, turn left on blue, and go straight through yellow.

Turns 8

GOAL: Enter the maze from the bottom, exit by the top.

RULES: You may retrace your path. Turn right on red, turn left on blue, and go straight through yellow.

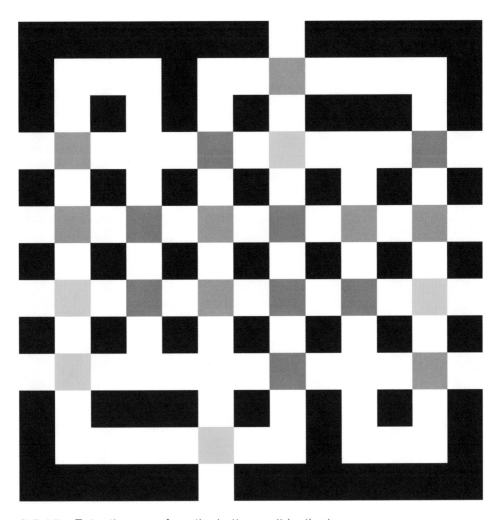

GOAL: Enter the maze from the bottom, exit by the top.
RULES: You may retrace your path. Turn right on red, turn left on blue, and go straight through yellow.

Turns 10

GOAL: Enter the maze from the bottom, exit by the top.
RULES: You may retrace your path. Turn right on red, turn left on blue, and go straight through yellow.

GOAL: Enter the maze from the bottom, exit by the top.
RULES: You may retrace your path. Turn right on red, turn left on blue,
and go straight through yellow.

Turns 12

GOAL: Enter the maze from the bottom, exit by the top.
RULES: You may retrace your path. Turn right on red, turn left on blue, and go straight through yellow.

GOAL: Enter the maze from the bottom, exit by the top.
RULES: You may retrace your path. Turn right on red, turn left on blue, and go straight through yellow.

Turns 14

GOAL: Enter the maze from the bottom, exit by the top.
RULES: You may retrace your path. Turn right on red, turn left on blue, and go straight through yellow.

GOAL: Enter the maze from the bottom, exit by the top.
RULES: You may retrace your path. Turn right on red, turn left on blue, and go straight through yellow.

Turns 16

GOAL: Enter the maze from the bottom, exit by the top.

RULES: You may retrace your path. Turn right on red, turn left on blue, and go straight through yellow.

GOAL: Enter the maze from the bottom, exit by the top.
RULES: You may retrace your path. Turn right on red, turn left on blue, and go straight through yellow.

Turns 18

GOAL: Enter the maze from the bottom, exit by the top.
RULES: You may retrace your path. Turn right on red, turn left on blue, and go straight through yellow.

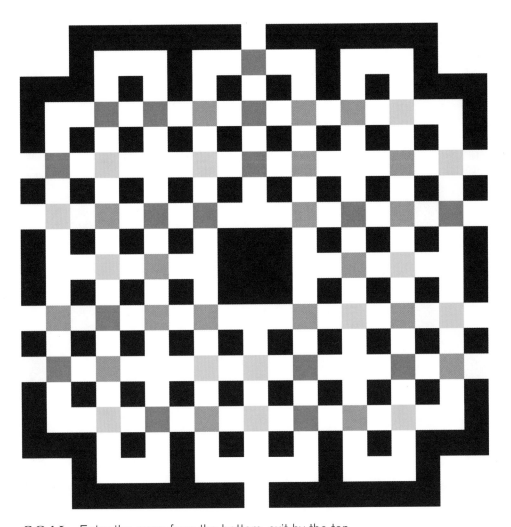

GOAL: Enter the maze from the bottom, exit by the top.
RULES: You may retrace your path. Turn right on red, turn left on blue, and go straight through yellow.

Turns 20

GOAL: Enter the maze from the bottom, exit by the top.

RULES: You may retrace your path. Turn right on red, turn left on blue, and go straight through yellow.

Sequence A

GOAL: Enter the maze through any of the available entrances, pass through all colored squares, and then exit the maze.

RULES: You may not retrace your paths. If the maze has only yellow squares, pass through each in any order. If the maze has red and blue squares, alternate between the two colors as you pass through the squares. In other words, you may not pass through two red squares or two blue squares in a row.

HINTS: If there is only one way into and out of a colored square, you know this section of path must be part of the solution. Piece together a solution using deduction.

GOAL: Enter the maze, pass through all yellow squares, and then exit the maze.

RULES: You may not retrace your path.

Sequence A 2

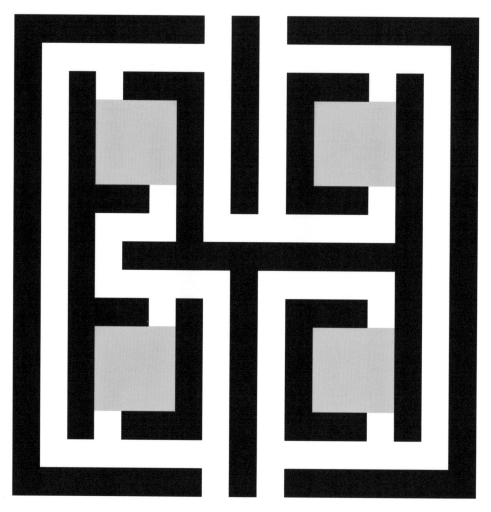

GOAL: Enter the maze, pass through all yellow squares, and then exit the maze.

RULES: You may not retrace your path.

GOAL: Enter the maze, pass through all yellow squares, and then exit the maze.

RULES: You may not retrace your path.

Sequence A 4

GOAL: Enter the maze, pass through all yellow squares, and then exit the maze.
RULES: You may not retrace your path.

GOAL: Enter the maze, pass through all yellow squares, and then exit the maze.

RULES: You may not retrace your path.

Sequence A 6

GOAL: Enter the maze, pass through all yellow squares, and then exit the maze.

RULES: You may not retrace your path.

GOAL: Enter the maze, pass through all yellow squares, and then exit the maze.

RULES: You may not retrace your path.

Sequence A 8

GOAL: Enter the maze, pass through all yellow squares, and then exit the maze.

RULES: You may not retrace your path.

GOAL: Enter the maze, pass through all yellow squares, and then exit the maze.

RULES: You may not retrace your path.

Sequence A 10

GOAL: Enter the maze, pass through all yellow squares, and then exit the maze.

RULES: You may not retrace your path.

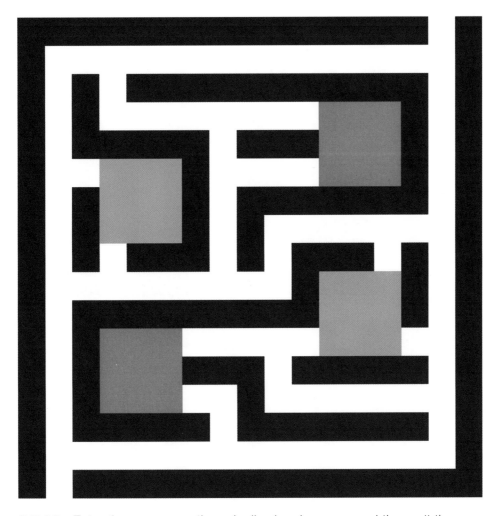

GOAL: Enter the maze, pass through all colored squares, and then exit the maze.

RULES: You may not retrace your path. Alternate between red squares and blue squares.

Sequence A 12

GOAL: Enter the maze, pass through all colored squares, and then exit the maze.

RULES: You may not retrace your path. Alternate between red squares and blue squares.

GOAL: Enter the maze, pass through all colored squares, and then exit the maze.
RULES: You may not retrace your path. Alternate between red squares and blue squares.

Sequence A 14

GOAL: Enter the maze, pass through all colored squares, and then exit the maze.

RULES: You may not retrace your path. Alternate between red squares and blue squares.

GOAL: Enter the maze, pass through all colored squares, and then exit the maze.

RULES: You may not retrace your path. Alternate between red squares and blue squares.

Sequence A 16

GOAL: Enter the maze, pass through all colored squares, and then exit the maze.

RULES: You may not retrace your path. Alternate between red squares and blue squares.

GOAL: Enter the maze, pass through all colored squares, and then exit the maze.

RULES: You may not retrace your path. Alternate between red squares and blue squares.

Sequence A 18

GOAL: Enter the maze, pass through all colored squares, and then exit the maze.

RULES: You may not retrace your path. Alternate between red squares and blue squares.

GOAL: Enter the maze, pass through all colored squares, and then exit the maze.

RULES: You may not retrace your path. Alternate between red squares and blue squares.

Sequence A 20

GOAL: Enter the maze, pass through all colored squares, and then exit the maze.
RULES: You may not retrace your path. Alternate between red squares and blue squares.

Sequence B

GOAL: Enter the maze through any of the available entrances, pass through all colored squares, and then exit the maze.

RULES: You may not retrace your paths. Pass through the colored squares in the order red, blue, yellow.

HINTS: Use the same reasoning as in Sequence A. Passing through the colors in the order red, blue, yellow going forward means that if you try solving the maze backward, you'll pass through the colors in the order yellow, blue, red. The last color visited before exiting the maze will always be yellow.

GOAL: Enter the maze, pass through all colored squares, and then exit the maze.
RULES: You may not retrace your path. Pass through squares in the order red, blue, yellow.

Sequence B 2

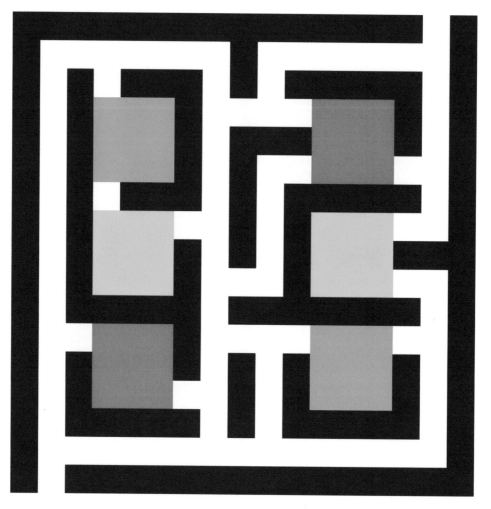

GOAL: Enter the maze, pass through all colored squares, and then exit the maze.
RULES: You may not retrace your path. Pass through squares in the order red, blue, yellow.

Sequence B 3

GOAL: Enter the maze, pass through all colored squares, and then exit the maze.
RULES: You may not retrace your path. Pass through squares in the order red, blue, yellow.

Sequence B 4

GOAL: Enter the maze, pass through all colored squares, and then exit the maze.
RULES: You may not retrace your path. Pass through squares in the order red, blue, yellow.

GOAL: Enter the maze, pass through all colored squares, and then exit the maze.
RULES: You may not retrace your path. Pass through squares in the order red, blue, yellow.

Sequence B 6

GOAL: Enter the maze, pass through all colored squares, and then exit the maze.
RULES: You may not retrace your path. Pass through squares in the order red, blue, yellow.

GOAL: Enter the maze, pass through all colored squares, and then exit the maze.
RULES: You may not retrace your path. Pass through squares in the order red, blue, yellow.

Sequence B 8

GOAL: Enter the maze, pass through all colored squares, and then exit the maze.
RULES: You may not retrace your path. Pass through squares in the order red, blue, yellow.

GOAL: Enter the maze, pass through all colored squares, and then exit the maze.
RULES: You may not retrace your path. Pass through squares in the order red, blue, yellow.

Sequence B 10

GOAL: Enter the maze, pass through all colored squares, and then exit the maze.
RULES: You may not retrace your path. Pass through squares in the order red, blue, yellow.

GOAL: Enter the maze, pass through all colored squares, and then exit the maze.
RULES: You may not retrace your path. Pass through squares in the order red, blue, yellow.

Sequence B 12

GOAL: Enter the maze, pass through all colored squares, and then exit the maze.
RULES: You may not retrace your path. Pass through squares in the order red, blue, yellow.

GOAL: Enter the maze, pass through all colored squares, and then exit the maze.

RULES: You may not retrace your path. Pass through squares in the order red, blue, yellow.

Sequence B 14

GOAL: Enter the maze, pass through all colored squares, and then exit the maze.
RULES: You may not retrace your path. Pass through squares in the order red, blue, yellow.

GOAL: Enter the maze, pass through all colored squares, and then exit the maze.

RULES: You may not retrace your path. Pass through squares in the order red, blue, yellow.

Sequence B 16

GOAL: Enter the maze, pass through all colored squares, and then exit the maze.
RULES: You may not retrace your path. Pass through squares in the order red, blue, yellow.

GOAL: Enter the maze, pass through all colored squares, and then exit the maze.
RULES: You may not retrace your path. Pass through squares in the order red, blue, yellow.

Sequence B 18

GOAL: Enter the maze, pass through all colored squares, and then exit the maze.

RULES: You may not retrace your path. Pass through squares in the order red, blue, yellow.

GOAL: Enter the maze, pass through all colored squares, and then exit the maze.
RULES: You may not retrace your path. Pass through squares in the order red, blue, yellow.

Sequence B 20

GOAL: Enter the maze, pass through all colored squares, and then exit the maze.
RULES: You may not retrace your path. Pass through squares in the order red, blue, yellow.

Two in a Row

GOAL: Enter the maze through any of the available entrances, pass through all colored squares once, and then exit the maze.

RULES: You may not retrace your paths. You may not pass through more than two squares of the same color in a row. Example: If the last two squares visited were red, the next square may not be red.

HINTS: Sometimes taking a diagonal path will make the maze impossible, regardless of the color of the squares.

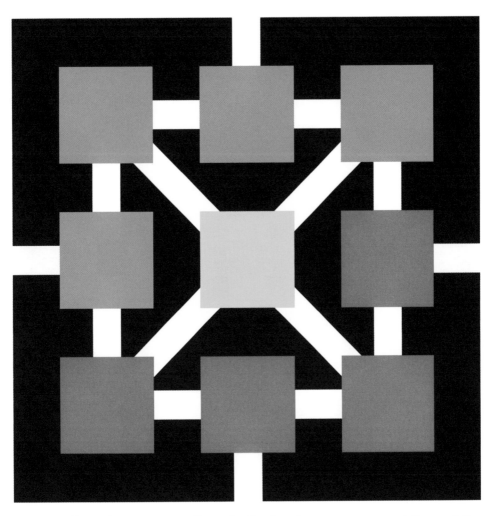

GOAL: Enter the maze, pass through all colored squares once, and then exit the maze.
RULES: You may not retrace your path. Do not pass through the same color three times in a row.

Two in a Row 2

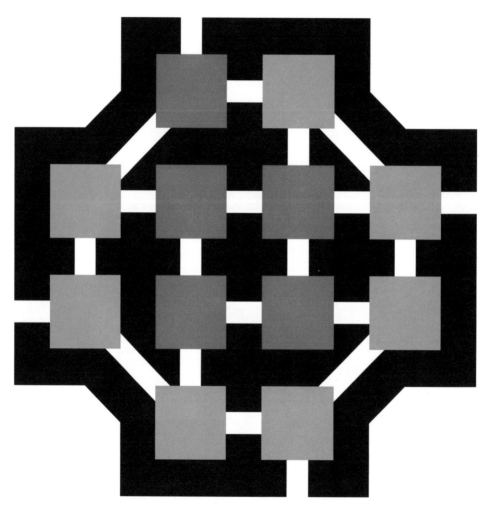

GOAL: Enter the maze, pass through all colored squares once, and then exit the maze.
RULES: You may not retrace your path. Do not pass through the same color three times in a row.

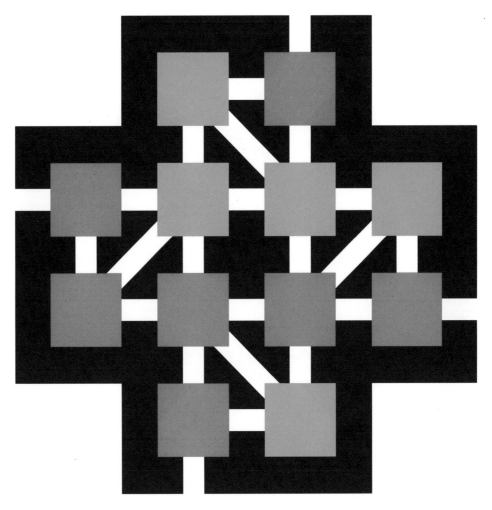

GOAL: Enter the maze, pass through all colored squares once, and then exit the maze.
RULES: You may not retrace your path. Do not pass through the same color three times in a row.

Two in a Row 4

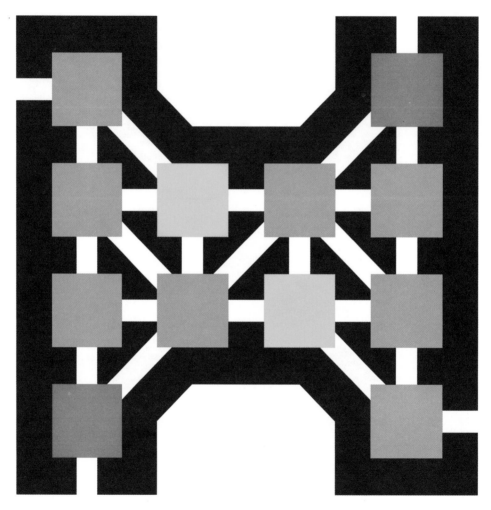

GOAL: Enter the maze, pass through all colored squares once, and then exit the maze.

RULES: You may not retrace your path. Do not pass through the same color three times in a row.

Two in a Row 5

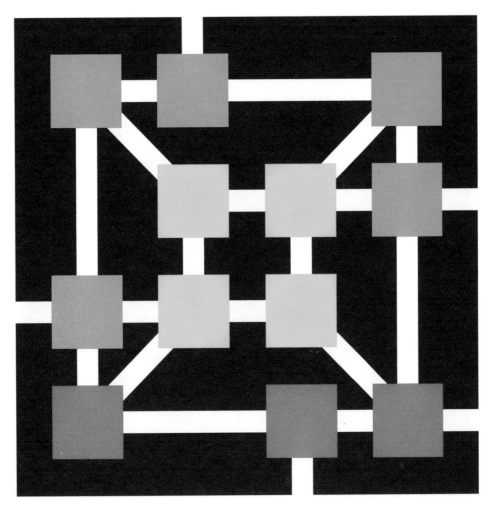

GOAL: Enter the maze, pass through all colored squares once, and then exit the maze.

RULES: You may not retrace your path. Do not pass through the same color three times in a row.

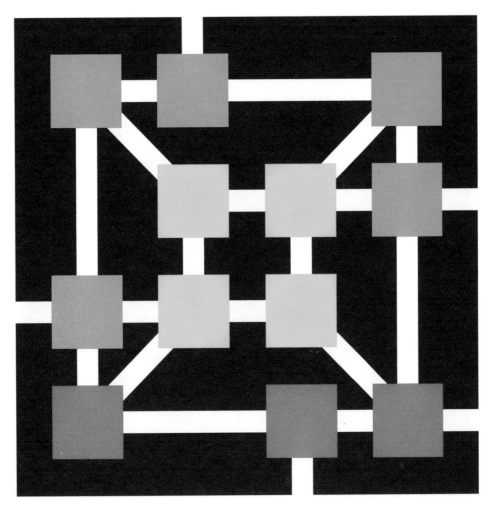

141

Two in a Row 6

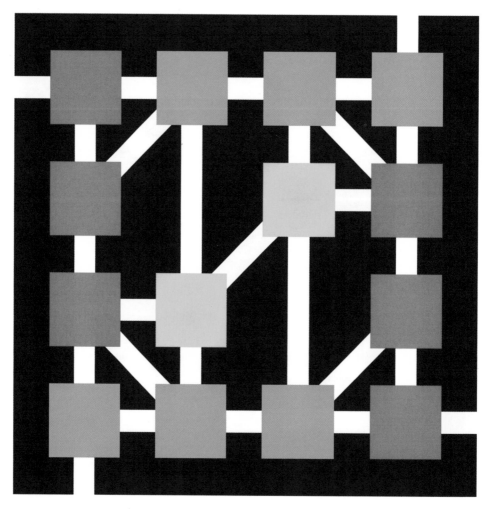

GOAL: Enter the maze, pass through all colored squares once, and then exit the maze.

RULES: You may not retrace your path. Do not pass through the same color three times in a row.

Two in a Row 7

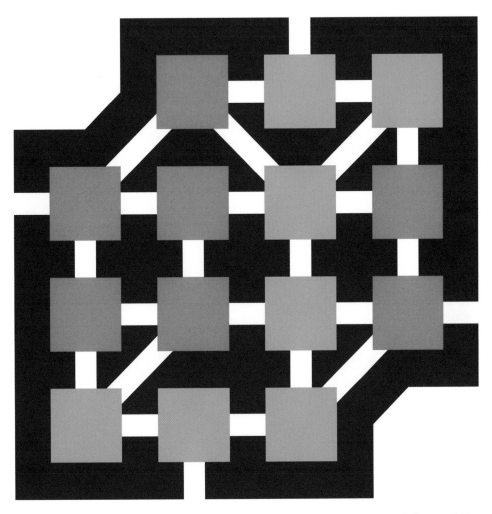

GOAL: Enter the maze, pass through all colored squares once, and then exit the maze.
RULES: You may not retrace your path. Do not pass through the same color three times in a row.

Two in a Row 8

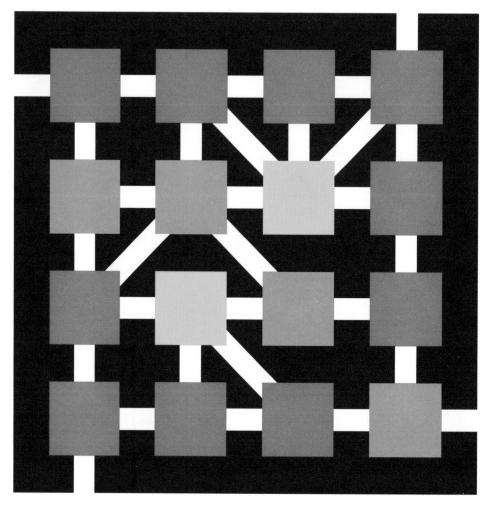

GOAL: Enter the maze, pass through all colored squares once, and then exit the maze.
RULES: You may not retrace your path. Do not pass through the same color three times in a row.

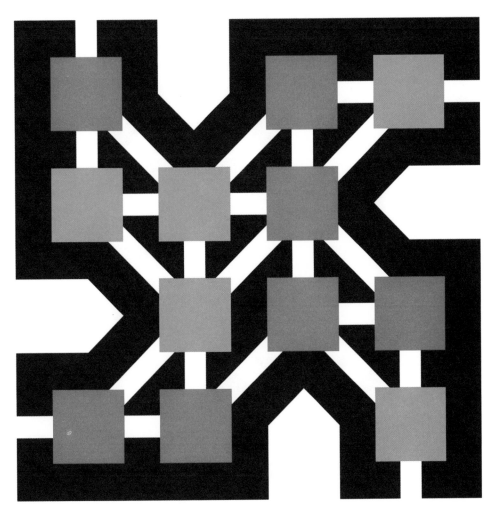

GOAL: Enter the maze, pass through all colored squares once, and then exit the maze.
RULES: You may not retrace your path. Do not pass through the same color three times in a row.

Two in a Row 10

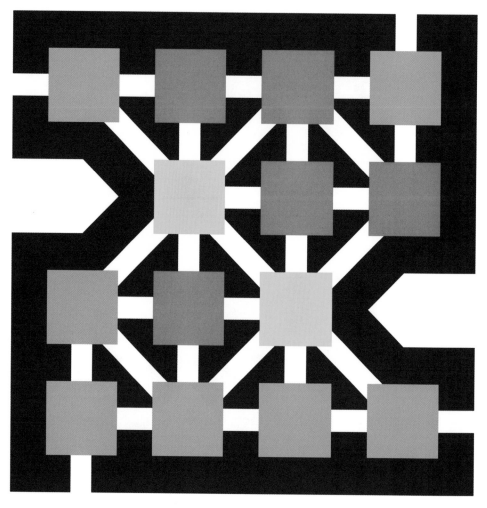

GOAL: Enter the maze, pass through all colored squares once, and then exit the maze.
RULES: You may not retrace your path. Do not pass through the same color three times in a row.

GOAL: Enter the maze, pass through all colored squares once, and then exit the maze.
RULES: You may not retrace your path. Do not pass through the same color three times in a row.

Two in a Row 12

GOAL: Enter the maze, pass through all colored squares once, and then exit the maze.
RULES: You may not retrace your path. Do not pass through the same color three times in a row.

GOAL: Enter the maze, pass through all colored squares once, and then exit the maze.
RULES: You may not retrace your path. Do not pass through the same color three times in a row.

Two in a Row 14

GOAL: Enter the maze, pass through all colored squares once, and then exit the maze.
RULES: You may not retrace your path. Do not pass through the same color three times in a row.

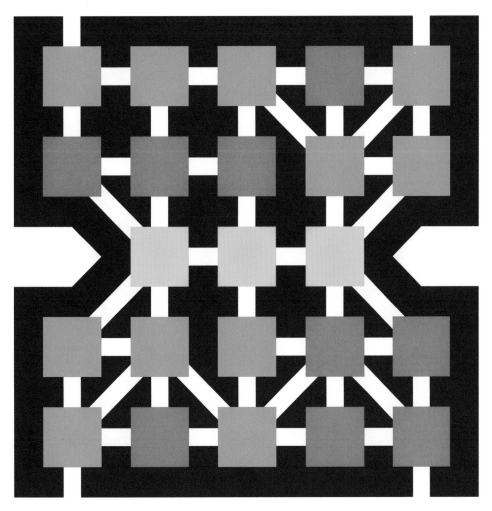

GOAL: Enter the maze, pass through all colored squares once, and then exit the maze.
RULES: You may not retrace your path. Do not pass through the same color three times in a row.

Two in a Row 16

GOAL: Enter the maze, pass through all colored squares once, and then exit the maze.
RULES: You may not retrace your path. Do not pass through the same color three times in a row.

Two in a Row 17

GOAL: Enter the maze, pass through all colored squares once, and then exit the maze.
RULES: You may not retrace your path. Do not pass through the same color three times in a row.

Two in a Row 18

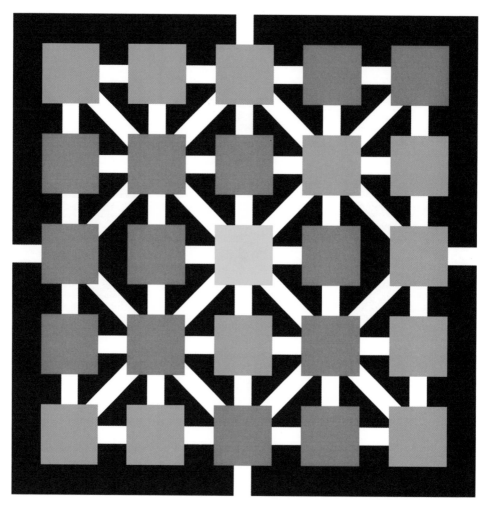

GOAL: Enter the maze, pass through all colored squares once, and then exit the maze.
RULES: You may not retrace your path. Do not pass through the same color three times in a row.

GOAL: Enter the maze, pass through all colored squares once, and then exit the maze.

RULES: You may not retrace your path. Do not pass through the same color three times in a row.

Two in a Row 20

GOAL: Enter the maze, pass through all colored squares once, and then exit the maze.
RULES: You may not retrace your path. Do not pass through the same color three times in a row.

Looped

GOAL: Create a single unbroken loop (like a long twisted rubber band) that passes through all open squares, including all white squares.

RULES: You may not visit any square more than once. You may pass from one square to another only if they share a common side (that is, no diagonal moves are allowed). You must alternate passing through red squares and blue squares (regardless of the number of white squares in between).

HINTS: Some squares have as many as six different ways to pass through them, but some squares have only one (for example, the squares in each corner). Much more than the other sections in this collection, this last section requires a great deal of deduction. Chance alone will not get you very far.

Looped 1

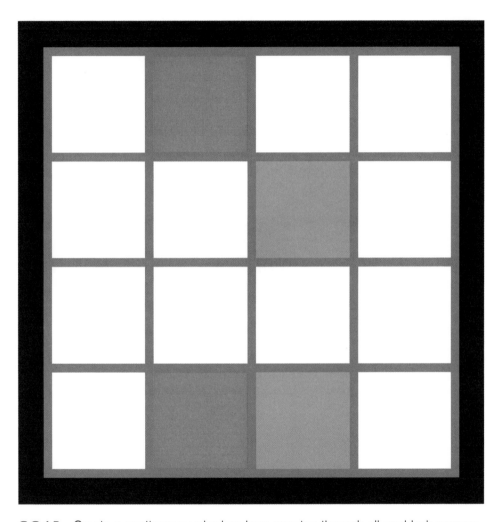

GOAL: Create a continuous unbroken loop, passing through all nonblack squares.
RULES: You may not visit a square more than once. You must alternate between red squares and blue squares, regardless of the number of white squares in between.

Looped 2

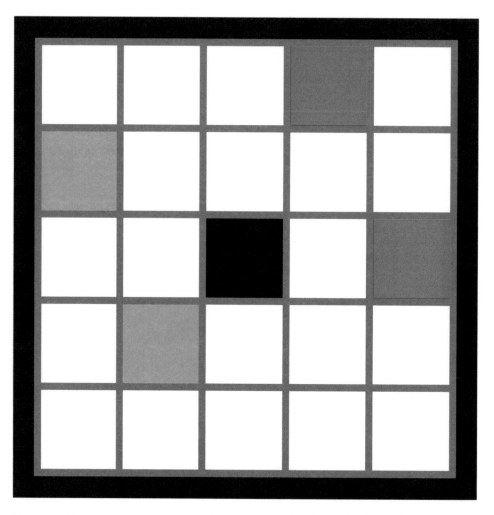

GOAL: Create a continuous unbroken loop, passing through all nonblack squares.
RULES: You may not visit a square more than once. You must alternate between red squares and blue squares, regardless of the number of white squares in between.

Looped 3

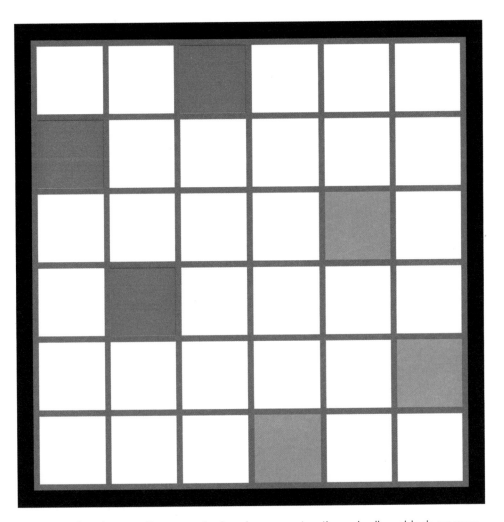

GOAL: Create a continuous unbroken loop, passing through all nonblack squares.
RULES: You may not visit a square more than once. You must alternate between red squares and blue squares, regardless of the number of white squares in between.

Looped 4

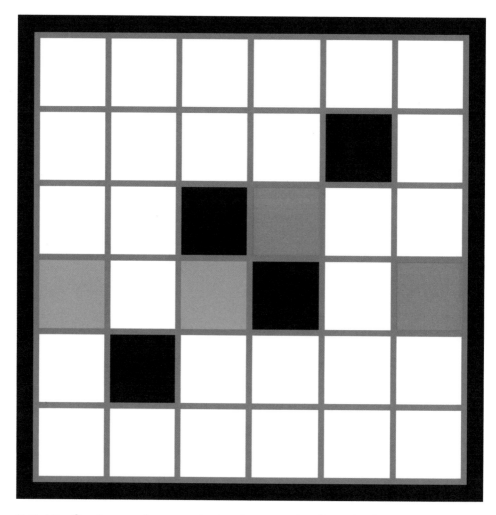

GOAL: Create a continuous unbroken loop, passing through all nonblack squares.
RULES: You may not visit a square more than once. You must alternate between red squares and blue squares, regardless of the number of white squares in between.

Looped 5

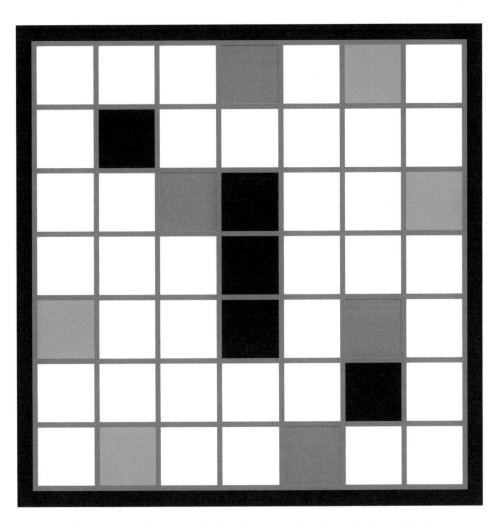

GOAL: Create a continuous unbroken loop, passing through all nonblack squares.
RULES: You may not visit a square more than once. You must alternate between red squares and blue squares, regardless of the number of white squares in between.

Looped 6

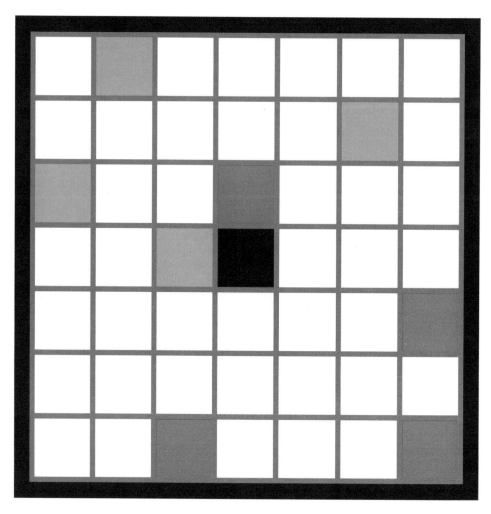

GOAL: Create a continuous unbroken loop, passing through all nonblack squares.
RULES: You may not visit a square more than once. You must alternate between red squares and blue squares, regardless of the number of white squares in between.

Looped 7

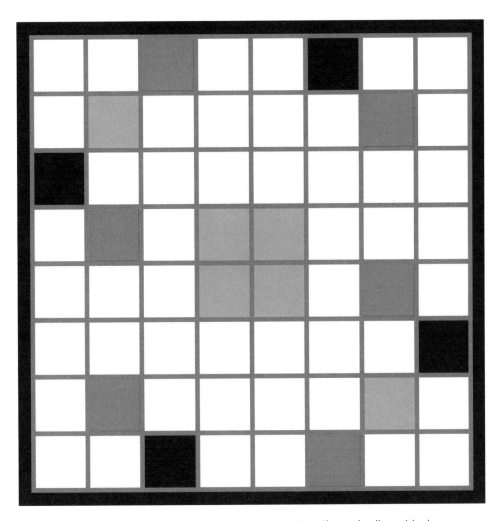

GOAL: Create a continuous unbroken loop, passing through all nonblack squares.
RULES: You may not visit a square more than once. You must alternate between red squares and blue squares, regardless of the number of white squares in between.

Looped 8

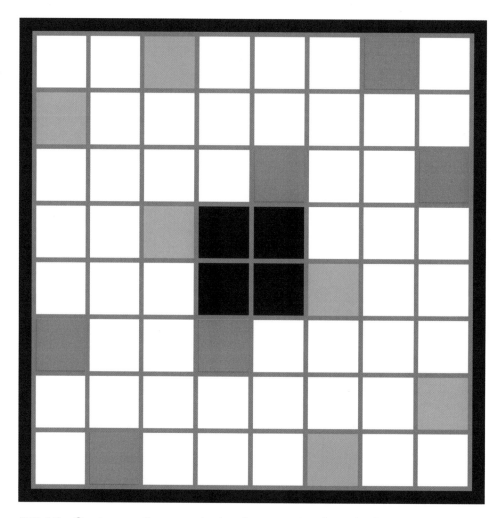

GOAL: Create a continuous unbroken loop, passing through all nonblack squares.
RULES: You may not visit a square more than once. You must alternate between red squares and blue squares, regardless of the number of white squares in between.

Looped 9

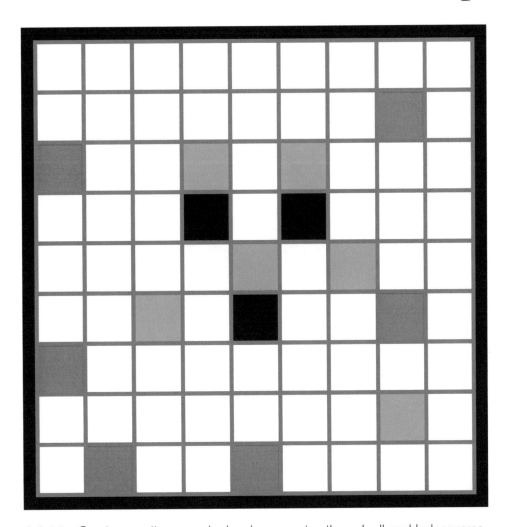

GOAL: Create a continuous unbroken loop, passing through all nonblack squares.
RULES: You may not visit a square more than once. You must alternate between red squares and blue squares, regardless of the number of white squares in between.

Looped 10

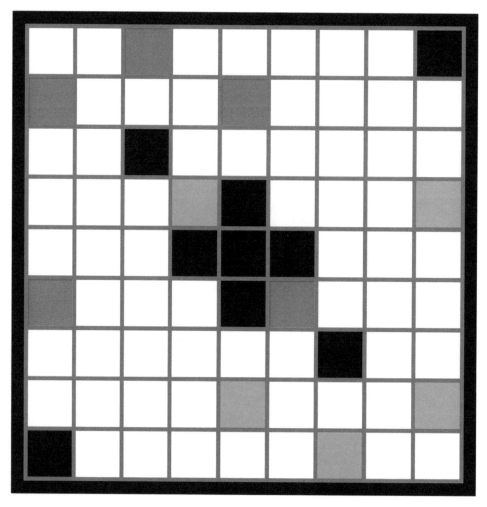

GOAL: Create a continuous unbroken loop, passing through all nonblack squares.
RULES: You may not visit a square more than once. You must alternate between
red squares and blue squares, regardless of the number of white squares in between.

Looped 11

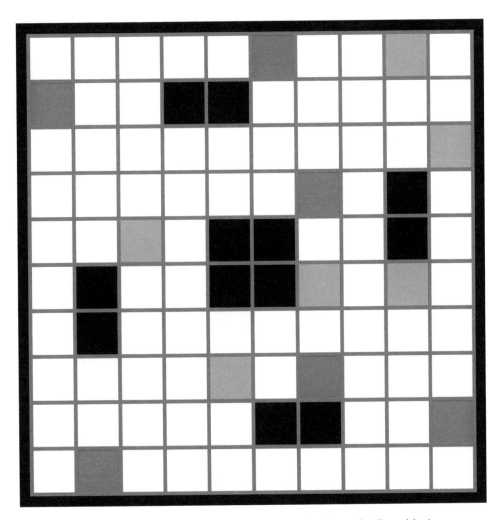

GOAL: Create a continuous unbroken loop, passing through all nonblack squares.
RULES: You may not visit a square more than once. You must alternate between red squares and blue squares, regardless of the number of white squares in between.

Looped 12

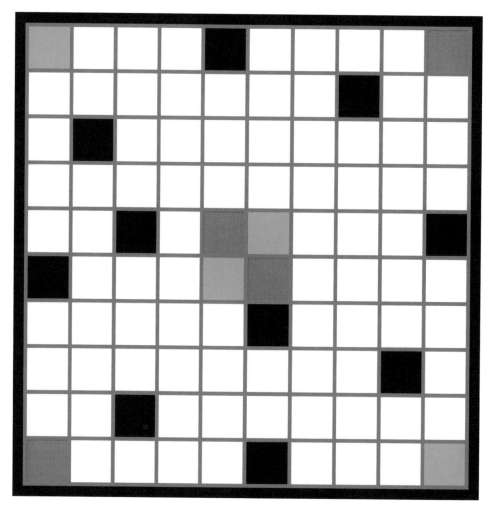

GOAL: Create a continuous unbroken loop, passing through all nonblack squares.

RULES: You may not visit a square more than once. You must alternate between red squares and blue squares, regardless of the number of white squares in between.

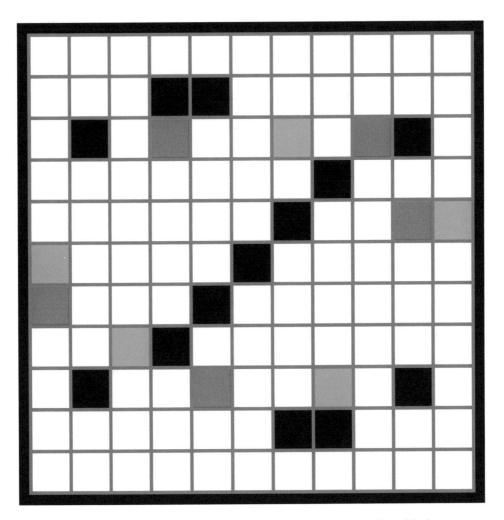

GOAL: Create a continuous unbroken loop, passing through all nonblack squares.
RULES: You may not visit a square more than once. You must alternate between red squares and blue squares, regardless of the number of white squares in between.

Looped 14

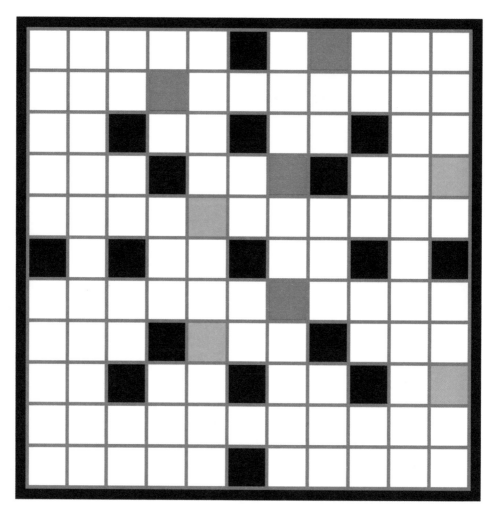

GOAL: Create a continuous unbroken loop, passing through all nonblack squares.
RULES: You may not visit a square more than once. You must alternate between red squares and blue squares, regardless of the number of white squares in between.

Looped 15

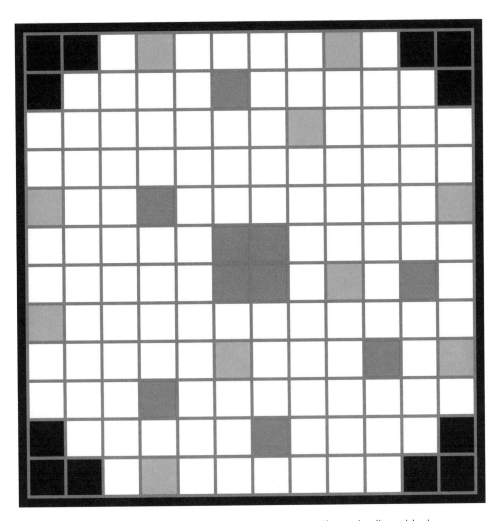

GOAL: Create a continuous unbroken loop, passing through all nonblack squares.

RULES: You may not visit a square more than once. You must alternate between red squares and blue squares, regardless of the number of white squares in between.

Looped 16

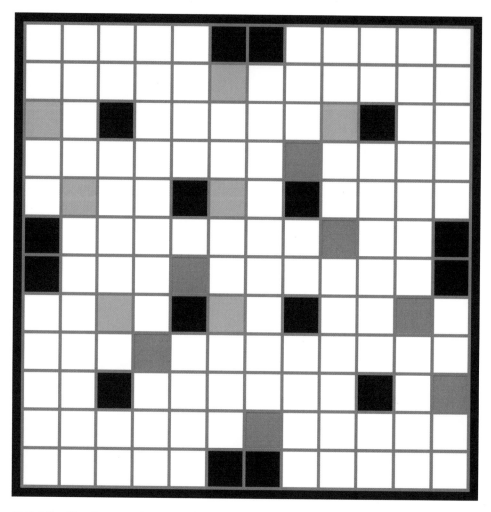

GOAL: Create a continuous unbroken loop, passing through all nonblack squares.
RULES: You may not visit a square more than once. You must alternate between red squares and blue squares, regardless of the number of white squares in between.

Looped 17

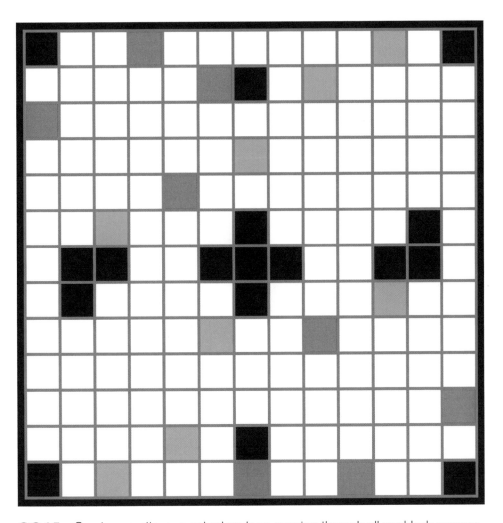

GOAL: Create a continuous unbroken loop, passing through all nonblack squares.
RULES: You may not visit a square more than once. You must alternate between red squares and blue squares, regardless of the number of white squares in between.

175

Looped 18

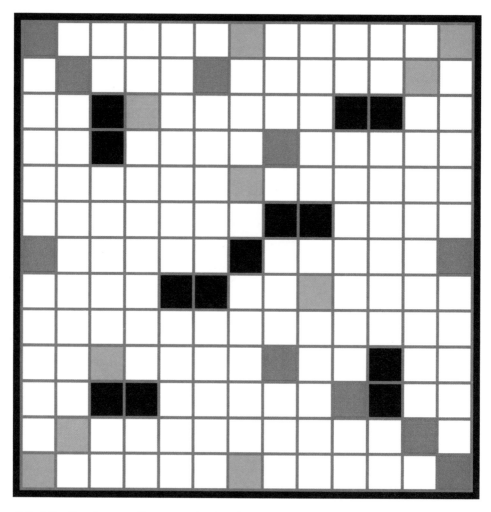

GOAL: Create a continuous unbroken loop, passing through all nonblack squares.
RULES: You may not visit a square more than once. You must alternate between red squares and blue squares, regardless of the number of white squares in between.

Looped 19

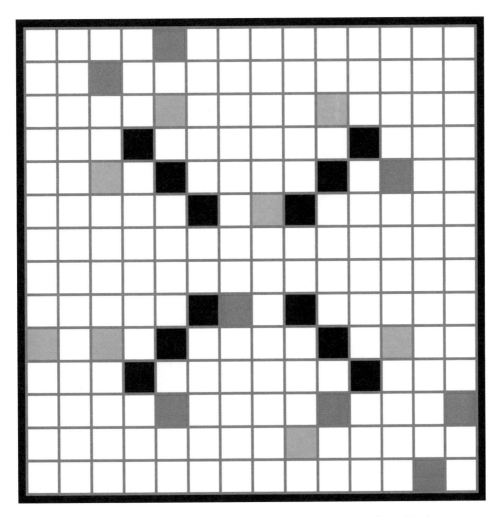

GOAL: Create a continuous unbroken loop, passing through all nonblack squares.
RULES: You may not visit a square more than once. You must alternate between red squares and blue squares, regardless of the number of white squares in between.

Looped 20

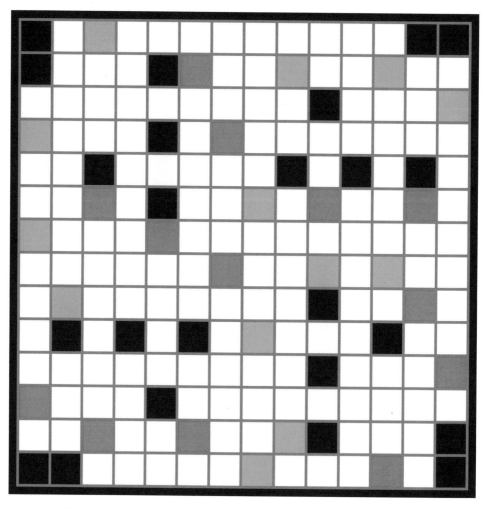

GOAL: Create a continuous unbroken loop, passing through all nonblack squares.

RULES: You may not visit a square more than once. You must alternate between red squares and blue squares, regardless of the number of white squares in between.

Solutions

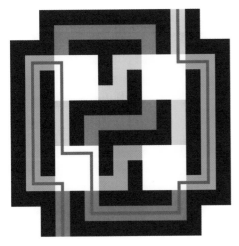

COLOR PATH 1, PAGE 5

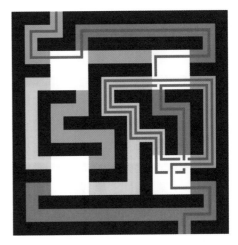

COLOR PATH 2, PAGE 6

COLOR PATH 3, PAGE 7

COLOR PATH 4, PAGE 8

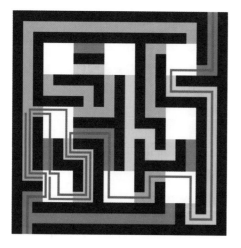

COLOR PATH 5, PAGE 9

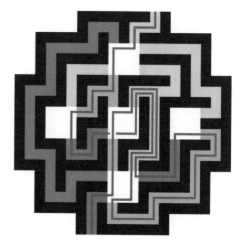

COLOR PATH 6, PAGE 10

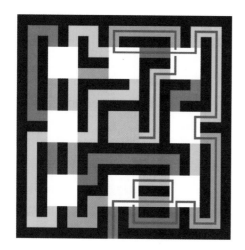

COLOR PATH 7, PAGE 11

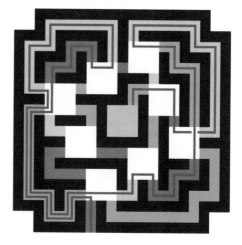

COLOR PATH 8, PAGE 12

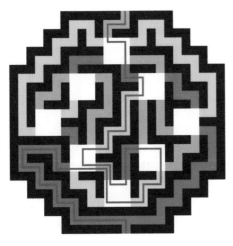

COLOR PATH 9, PAGE 13

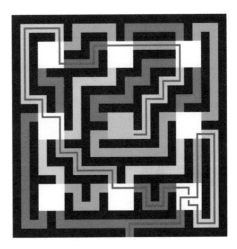

COLOR PATH 10, PAGE 14

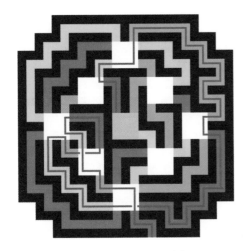

COLOR PATH 11, PAGE 15

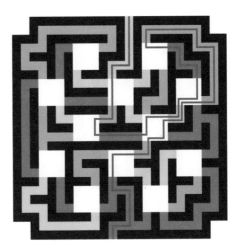

COLOR PATH 12, PAGE 16

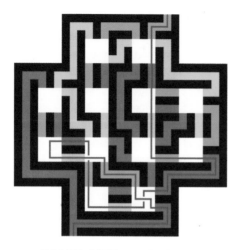

COLOR PATH 13, PAGE 17

COLOR PATH 14, PAGE 18

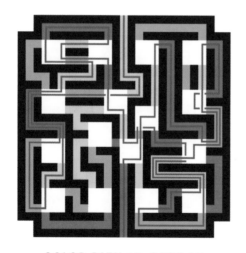

COLOR PATH 15, PAGE 19

COLOR PATH 16, PAGE 20

COLOR PATH 17, PAGE 21

COLOR PATH 18, PAGE 22

COLOR PATH 19, PAGE 23

COLOR PATH 20, PAGE 24

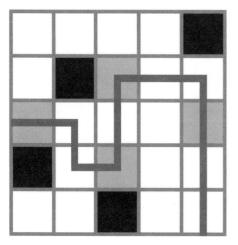

STRAIGHT 1, PAGE 27

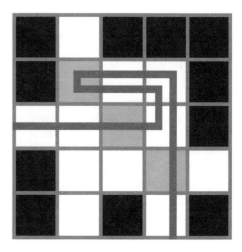

STRAIGHT 2, PAGE 28

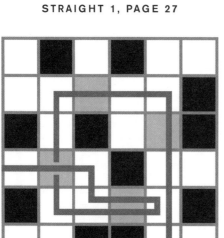

STRAIGHT 3, PAGE 29

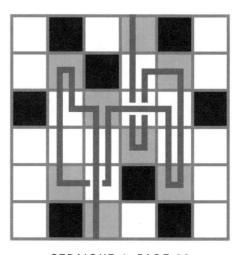

STRAIGHT 4, PAGE 30

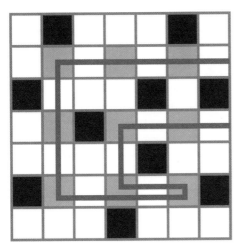

STRAIGHT 5, PAGE 31

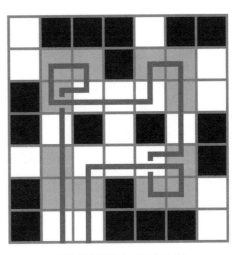

STRAIGHT 6, PAGE 32

STRAIGHT 7, PAGE 33

STRAIGHT 8, PAGE 34

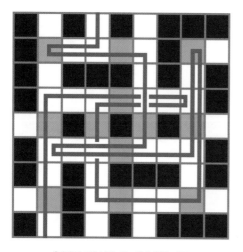

STRAIGHT 9, PAGE 35

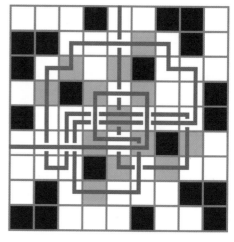

STRAIGHT 10, PAGE 36

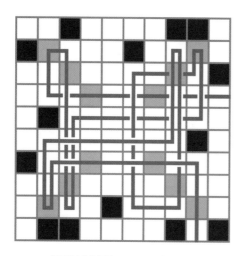

STRAIGHT 11, PAGE 37

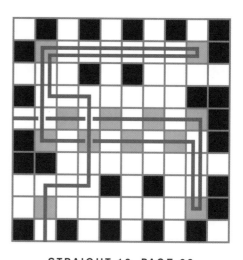

STRAIGHT 12, PAGE 38

STRAIGHT 13, PAGE 39

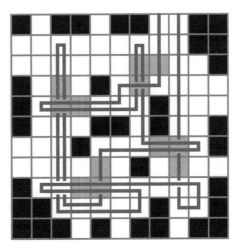

STRAIGHT 14, PAGE 40

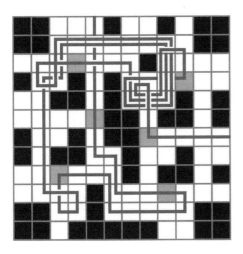

STRAIGHT 15, PAGE 41

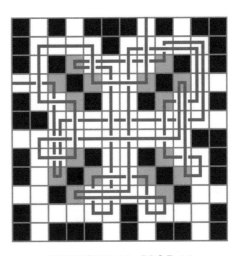

STRAIGHT 16, PAGE 42

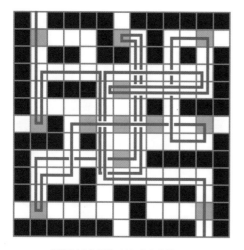

STRAIGHT 17, PAGE 43

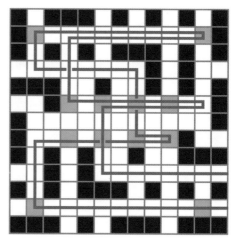

STRAIGHT 18, PAGE 44

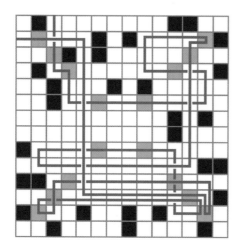

STRAIGHT 19, PAGE 45

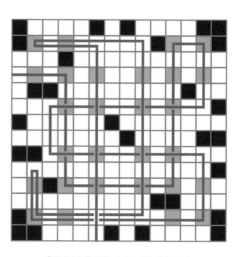

STRAIGHT 20, PAGE 46

FLOW 1, PAGE 49

FLOW 2, PAGE 50

FLOW 3, PAGE 51

FLOW 4, PAGE 52

FLOW 5, PAGE 53

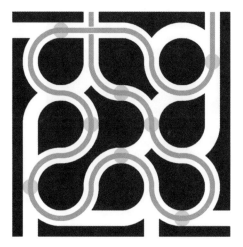

FLOW 6, PAGE 54

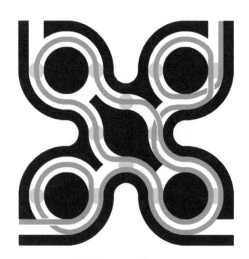

FLOW 7, PAGE 55

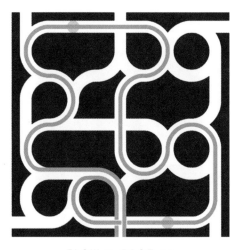

FLOW 8, PAGE 56

FLOW 9, PAGE 57

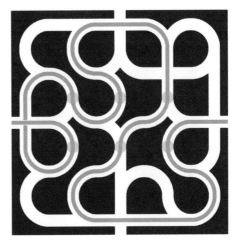

FLOW 10, PAGE 58

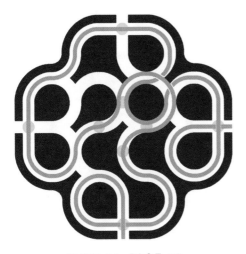

FLOW 11, PAGE 59

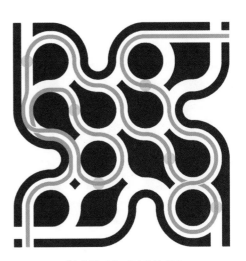

FLOW 12, PAGE 60

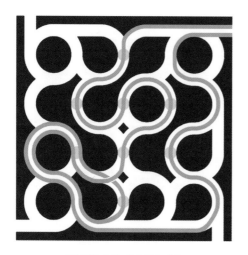

FLOW 13, PAGE 61

FLOW 14, PAGE 62

FLOW 15, PAGE 63

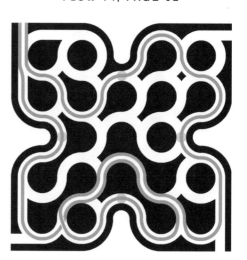

FLOW 16, PAGE 64

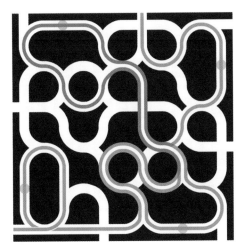

FLOW 17, PAGE 65

FLOW 18, PAGE 66

FLOW 19, PAGE 67

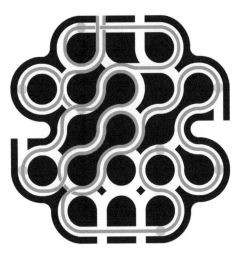

FLOW 20, PAGE 68

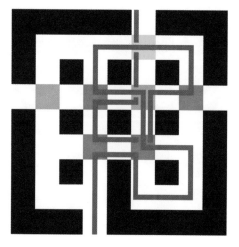

TURNS 1, PAGE 71

TURNS 2, PAGE 72

TURNS 3, PAGE 73

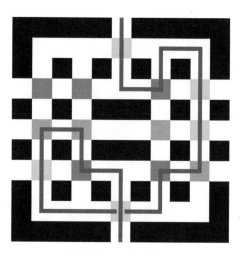

TURNS 4, PAGE 74

TURNS 5, PAGE 75

TURNS 6, PAGE 76

TURNS 7, PAGE 77

TURNS 8, PAGE 78

TURNS 9, PAGE 79

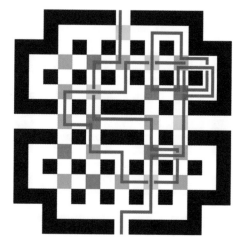

TURNS 10, PAGE 80

TURNS 11, PAGE 81

TURNS 12, PAGE 82

TURNS 13, PAGE 83

TURNS 14, PAGE 84

TURNS 15, PAGE 85

TURNS 16, PAGE 86

TURNS 17, PAGE 87

TURNS 18, PAGE 88

TURNS 19, PAGE 89

TURNS 20, PAGE 90

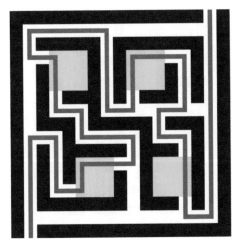

SEQUENCE A 1, PAGE 93

SEQUENCE A 2, PAGE 94

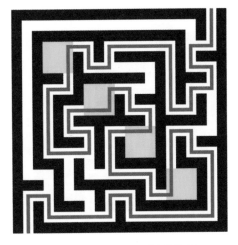

SEQUENCE A 3, PAGE 95

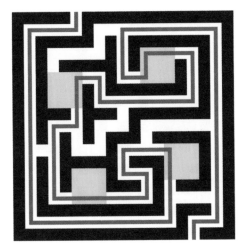

SEQUENCE A 4, PAGE 96

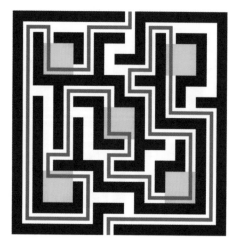

SEQUENCE A 5, PAGE 97

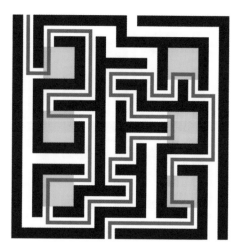

SEQUENCE A 6, PAGE 98

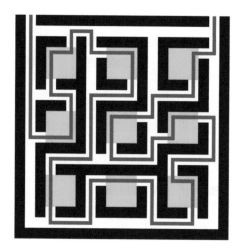

SEQUENCE A 7, PAGE 99

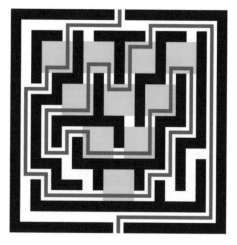

SEQUENCE A 8, PAGE 100

SEQUENCE A 9, PAGE 101

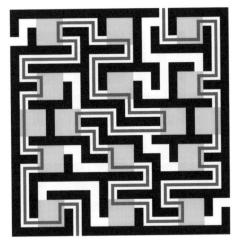

SEQUENCE A 10, PAGE 102

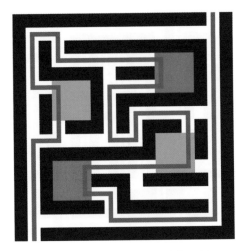

SEQUENCE A 11, PAGE 103

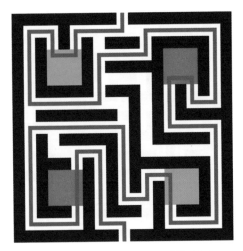

SEQUENCE A 12, PAGE 104

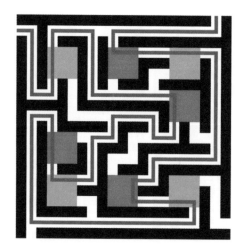

SEQUENCE A 13, PAGE 105

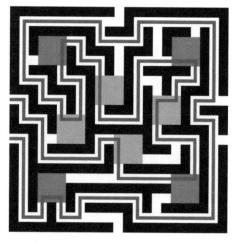

SEQUENCE A 14, PAGE 106

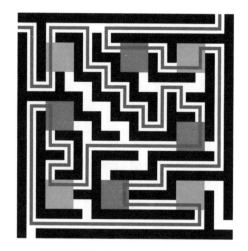

SEQUENCE A 15, PAGE 107

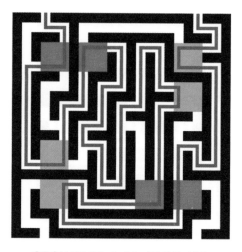

SEQUENCE A 16, PAGE 108

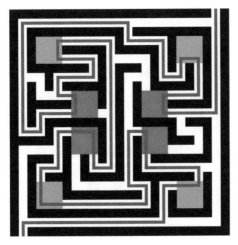

SEQUENCE A 17, PAGE 109

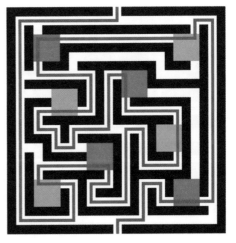

SEQUENCE A 18, PAGE 110

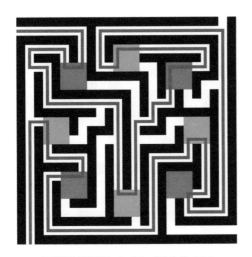

SEQUENCE A 19, PAGE 111

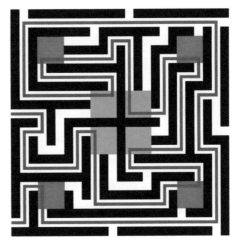

SEQUENCE A 20, PAGE 112

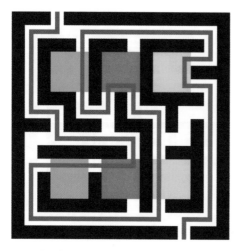

SEQUENCE B 1, PAGE 115

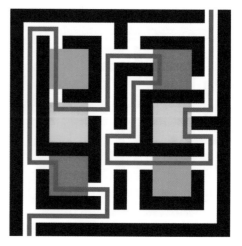

SEQUENCE B 2, PAGE 116

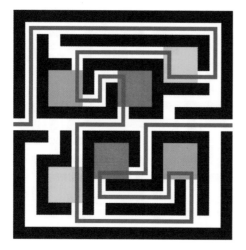

SEQUENCE B 3, PAGE 117

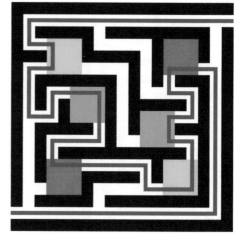

SEQUENCE B 4, PAGE 118

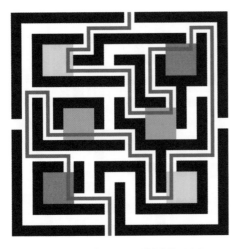

SEQUENCE B 5, PAGE 119

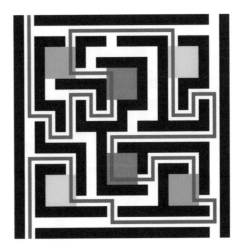

SEQUENCE B 6, PAGE 120

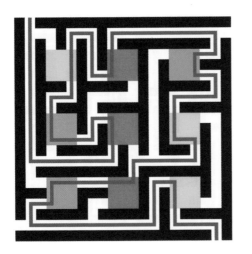

SEQUENCE B 7, PAGE 121

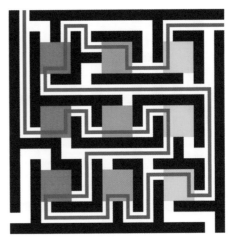

SEQUENCE B 8, PAGE 122

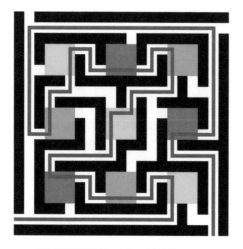

SEQUENCE B 9, PAGE 123

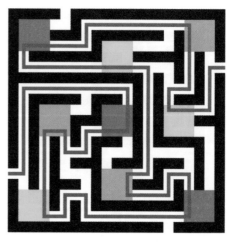

SEQUENCE B 10, PAGE 124

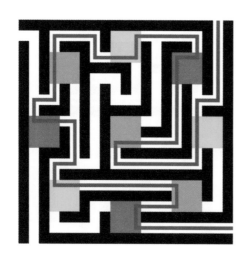

SEQUENCE B 11, PAGE 125

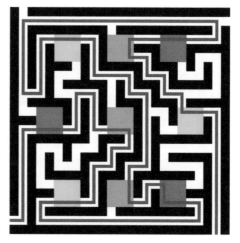

SEQUENCE B 12, PAGE 126

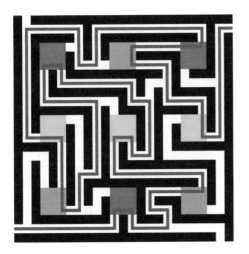

SEQUENCE B 13, PAGE 127

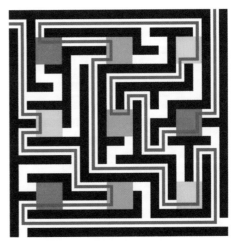

SEQUENCE B 14, PAGE 128

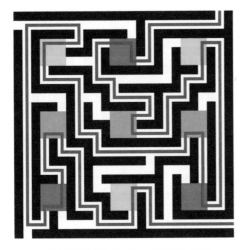

SEQUENCE B 15, PAGE 129

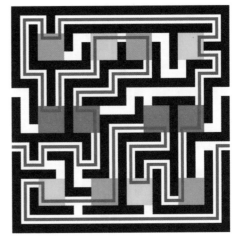

SEQUENCE B 16, PAGE 130

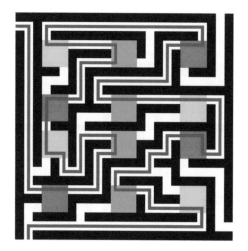

SEQUENCE B 17, PAGE 131

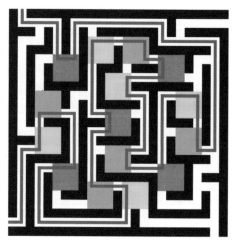

SEQUENCE B 18, PAGE 132

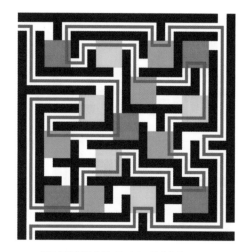

SEQUENCE B 19, PAGE 133

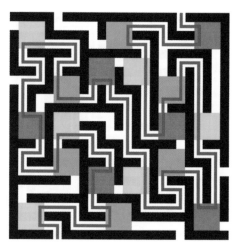

SEQUENCE B 20, PAGE 134

TWO IN A ROW 1, PAGE 137

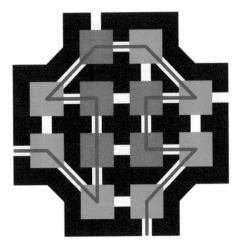

TWO IN A ROW 2, PAGE 138

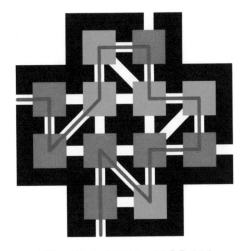

TWO IN A ROW 3, PAGE 139

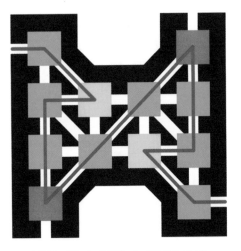

TWO IN A ROW 4, PAGE 140

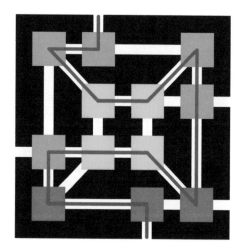

TWO IN A ROW 5, PAGE 141

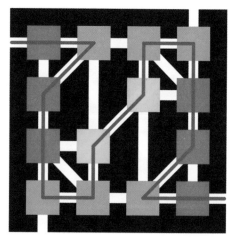

TWO IN A ROW 6, PAGE 142

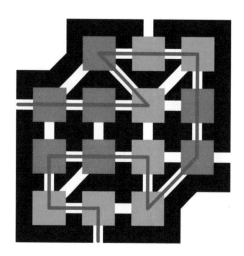

TWO IN A ROW 7, PAGE 143

TWO IN A ROW 8, PAGE 144

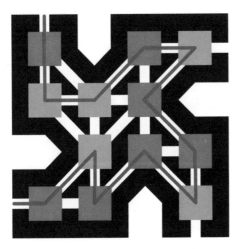

TWO IN A ROW 9, PAGE 145

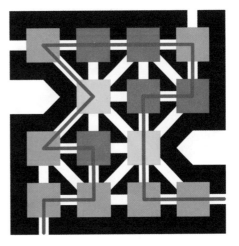

TWO IN A ROW 10, PAGE 146

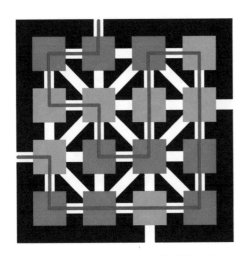

TWO IN A ROW 11, PAGE 147

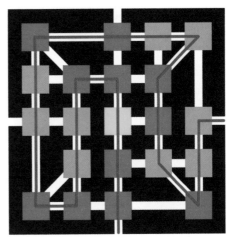

TWO IN A ROW 12, PAGE 148

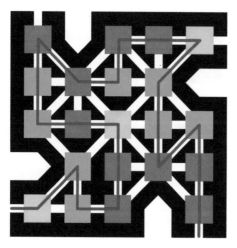

TWO IN A ROW 13, PAGE 149

TWO IN A ROW 14, PAGE 150

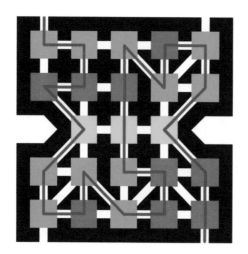

TWO IN A ROW 15, PAGE 151

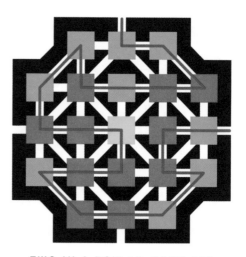

TWO IN A ROW 16, PAGE 152

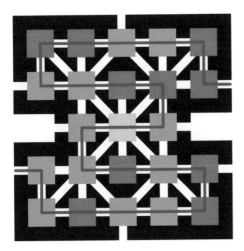

TWO IN A ROW 17, PAGE 153

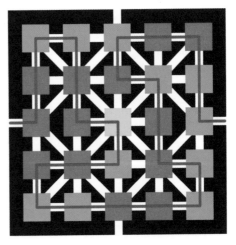

TWO IN A ROW 18, PAGE 154

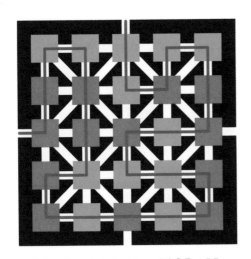

TWO IN A ROW 19, PAGE 155

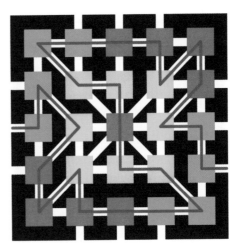

TWO IN A ROW 20, PAGE 156

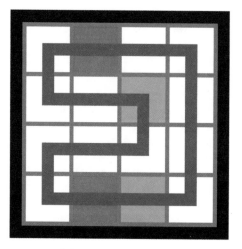

LOOPED 1, PAGE 159

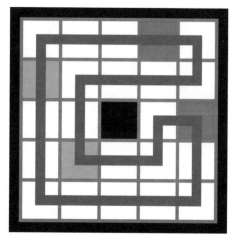

LOOPED 2, PAGE 160

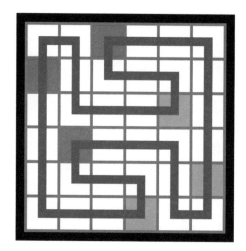

LOOPED 3, PAGE 161

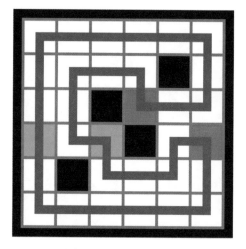

LOOPED 4, PAGE 162

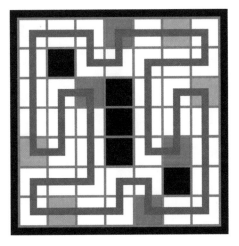

LOOPED 5, PAGE 163

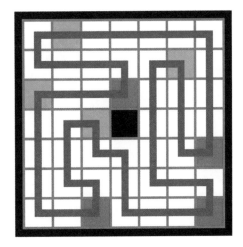

LOOPED 6, PAGE 164

LOOPED 7, PAGE 165

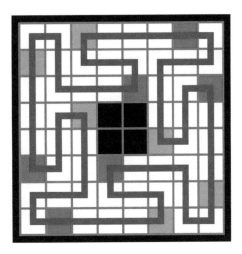

LOOPED 8, PAGE 166

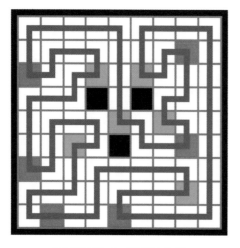

LOOPED 9, PAGE 167

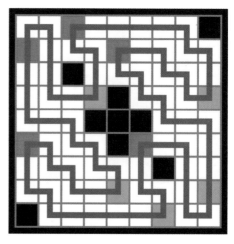

LOOPED 10, PAGE 168

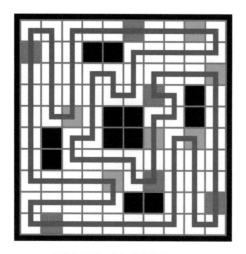

LOOPED 11, PAGE 169

LOOPED 12, PAGE 170

LOOPED 13, PAGE 171

LOOPED 14, PAGE 172

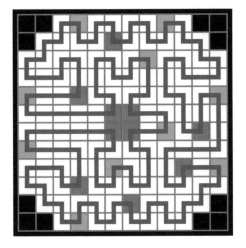

LOOPED 15, PAGE 173

LOOPED 16, PAGE 174

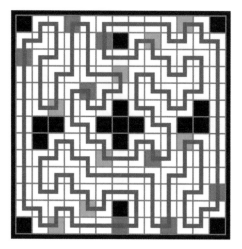

LOOPED 17, PAGE 175

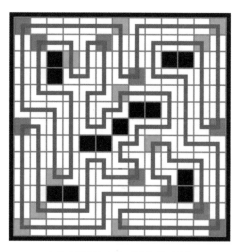

LOOPED 18, PAGE 176

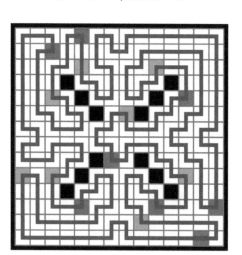

LOOPED 19, PAGE 177

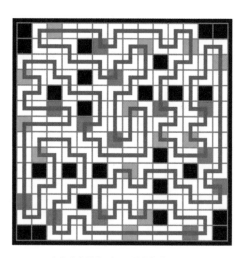

LOOPED 20, PAGE 178